MAKING NONFICTION FROM SCRATCH

Making Nonfiction From Scratch

RALPH FLETCHER

Stenhouse Publishers

Portland, Maine

Stenhouse Publishers
www.stenhouse.com

Credits
Pages 15–16: "It's Snack Time in the Cosmos" from the *New York Times*, February 18, 2014 © 2014 The New York Times. All rights reserved. Used by permission and protected by the Copyright Laws of the United States. The printing, copying, redistribution, or retransmission of this Content without express written permission is prohibited.
Pages 79–80: "Olympics: Skeleton Plunges Face-First Back into the Winter Games" from the *New York Times*, February 18, 2002 © 2002 The New York Times. All rights reserved. Used by permission and protected by the Copyright Laws of the United States. The printing, copying, redistribution, or retransmission of this Content without express written permission is prohibited.

Library of Congress Cataloging-in-Publication Data
Names: Fletcher, Ralph J.
Title: Making nonfiction from scratch / Ralph Fletcher.
Description: Portland, Maine : Stenhouse Publishers, [2016]
Identifiers: LCCN 2015026479| ISBN 9781625310125 (pbk. : alk. paper) | ISBN 9781625310842 (ebook)
Subjects: LCSH: Authorship. | Prose literature--Authorship. | Creative nonfiction--Authorship. | Reportage literature--Authorship.
Classification: LCC PN145 .F56 2016 | DDC 808.02--dc23 LC record available at http://lccn.loc.gov/2015026479

Cover and interior design by Lucian Burg, Lu Design Studios, Portland, ME
www.ludesignstudios.com

Manufactured in the United States of America

PRINTED ON 30% PCW
RECYCLED PAPER

21 20 19 18 17 16 15   9 8 7 6 5 4 3 2 1

for JoAnn—

woman with a big heart
and the most inquisitive mind
I know

CONTENTS

Acknowledgments

It all started with **Philippa Stratton, as it often does. Philippa** edited my very first professional book many years ago. She read early drafts of this book and made several important suggestions. I revised the manuscript and thought things were going swimmingly until one day we had lunch at Street Restaurant in Portsmouth, New Hampshire. I had just popped one of their delectable curry fries (crispy fries drizzled with curry mayo and served with a side of curry ketchup) into my mouth when Philippa mentioned that she'd be retiring at the end of the year.

"You'll be working with someone else after that," she said casually. I laughed; unfortunately, she wasn't kidding.

Working with an editor is personal and intimate. The realization that I would have to abruptly change partners and attempt the editor-author dance with someone unfamiliar made me nervous and disoriented.

But my new editor, Maureen Barbieri, turned out to be great. She wasn't exactly "new," either; we go back a few years. Maureen showered me with so much thumbs-up enthusiasm, it was almost like unconditional book-love. Her good vibrations helped me stay on course and finish the book.

I am grateful to a number of people who made important contributions to this book, especially Louise Borden, Bob Crongeyer, Mary Lou Williams, Caroline Andros, Kelly Milner Halls, Ryan Prescott, Penny Kittle, David Perkins, Cyrene Wells, Lester Laminack,

Franki Sibberson, Stef Harvey, Ron Berger, Larry Dane Brimner, and Roxie Munro. Thanks also to Jay Kilburn, Chris Downey, and the entire Stenhouse team.

I feel lucky to have worked with so many skilled editors who helped me shape my other nonfiction books. This list includes Toby Gordon, Holly Price, Lois Bridges, Christy Ottaviano, and Dinah Stevenson, just to name a few. Every one of these editors gave me many valuable writing conferences.

I've been inspired by many nonfiction writers for children and for adult readers: Aliki Brandenburg, Joanna Cole, Russell Freedman, Gail Gibbons, Seymour Simon, Steve Jenkins, Jim Murphy, John McPhee, Diane Ackerman, and Tom Wolfe, just to name a few.

Thanks to Chris Crutcher, Mike McCormick, and Katie Wood Ray.

I feel lucky that my wife, JoAnn, and I share a keen interest in the physical world. The eclectic list of subjects we have explored together just keeps growing: rock-hounding, Thai cooking, teaching writing, grandparenting, Buddhism, birding, gardening, composting . . .

The deepest roots for my interest in nonfiction can be found in my childhood. When I was a little boy my mother took my siblings and me on walks she called "Signs of Spring." She drew our attention to buds and tiny grass seedlings, and helped us tune in to the magic. That's perhaps the greatest thing I inherited from my parents—a fascination with the natural world. My brothers and sisters got that, too. I have an indelible memory of being at the beach with my brother Tom and my young sons. Tom had found an unusual rock and called them to come look at it. Was it a fossil? A crystal? They raced over, their small heads drawn to the stone in his hand like iron to a powerful magnet. I loved watching my kids fall in love with the natural world, because that sense of wonder was an indelible part of my childhood, too, and it infuses all my writing even to this day.

COOKING FROM SCRATCH

During my freshman year of college I brought a friend home for Thanksgiving. He watched in rapt fascination as my mother rolled out the dough for an apple pie on the counter.

"What?" my mother asked, puzzled by his interest.

"I've never seen anybody make a homemade pie before," he admitted.

"Never?" My mother was flabbergasted. "But . . . where did you get your pies?"

"I don't know." His expression turned sheepish. "From the store, I guess."

This anecdote may sound extreme, but in this prefab, ready-made, hurry-up, grab-'n'-go world I suspect you could find many people who would acknowledge that they had never feasted on homemade pies, bread, jam, or spaghetti sauce when they were growing up.

When our boys were little they liked waffles for breakfast. For a time I used one of those ready-made pancake mixes like Bisquick. You only had to add milk, eggs, and oil to make the batter. But mornings at our house were hectic, and I found that even that took too much time. Soon I got into the habit of buying premade Eggo waffles, found in the frozen food section at the supermarket. Now there was no need to mix any batter. All you had to do was drop the frozen waffles into the toaster, warm them up, and voila! They were ready for syrup and butter. Other than a faint cardboardy flavor, they didn't taste half-bad.

Then one day I read an alarming article about the paltry nutritional value of prepackaged foods. After that I resolved to start making waffles the right way. I got up early so I could mix the batter: milk, butter, salt, sugar, two eggs, and four teaspoons baking powder. It wasn't as difficult as I expected. That morning I served them the real deal—authentic, old-school waffles that were made from scratch. I felt a glow of paternal pride as I watched my kids eat them. But after a few moments I began to discern a distinct lack of enthusiasm in Joseph, our youngest.

"Tasty, huh?" I asked him. "What do you think?"

"It's . . . okay," he muttered.

"Just 'okay'?"

Joseph shrugged. "I like the Eggo waffles better. I guess I'm more used to that taste."

Observe a classroom full of kids writing nonfiction and you run into a glaring paradox. On the one hand it's apparent that kids genuinely like this genre. Many students (often boys) who sleepwalk through personal narrative suddenly wake up and get excited when invited to write about spiders, volcanoes, or killer whales. When it comes to nonfiction, teachers don't have to work very hard to motivate students. Kids respond to the indisputable "truthiness" of nonfiction: The *Titanic* actually did hit an iceberg, which damaged its hull and caused the mighty ship to sink in the icy waters of the North Atlantic. Fifteen hundred passengers lost their lives. Cicadas actually do stay buried in the ground for seventeen years before they emerge by the billions. Nonfiction taps into the senses of wonder and curiosity that are enduring hallmarks of childhood.

So with this genre we start with an intrinsic buy-in from students. On the other hand, I see an awful lot of formulaic nonfiction writing in the schools I visit. Nonfiction is the writing genre most typically "done to" students. We channel students into a particular curricular area whether they like it or not. We organize their writing for them, directing them to follow rubrics and use detailed prewriting outlines and graphic organizers. We teach them our system for taking notes and doing research. We tell students, "Your final report must include _____, and _____, and _____." No wonder students feel confined! No wonder so much of their nonfiction writing lacks energy and voice.

Welcome to nonfiction writing: our most prepackaged genre. My kids had eaten so many frozen waffles, they had come to believe that waffles were supposed to have that slightly chemical, cardboardy taste. In a similar way, nonfiction writing has been taught in such a way that many people—teachers, administrators, parents, students— have come to believe that this is the way it's supposed to sound and feel and taste. But I think—I *know*—we can do a lot better.

Real-World Nonfiction: A Moving Train

Seeing so much formulaic nonfiction writing in school puzzles me because in the real world things are moving in the opposite direction. In the world at large there's an exciting renaissance of nonfiction. This genre is busy being reborn, rapidly reinventing itself in a more playful, less rigid and scripted form. Twenty years ago the options were quite limited for anyone who wanted to learn about a particular subject: a newspaper, a nonfiction book, a feature article in a magazine, or an entry found in an encyclopedia. Today a rich variety of new formats are readily available. If you want to learn about something you can

- download a podcast and listen to it at your convenience.
- watch a YouTube video.
- visit a website, blog, or electronic mailing list.
- listen to a TED Talk where you can hear an expert insider talking about a particular topic.
- immerse yourself in a multimedia newspaper article. I say *immerse* because *read* does not seem sufficient to describe what it's like to experience this evolving media. Check out "Snow Fall: The Avalanche at Tunnel Creek" by John Branch. http://www.nytimes.com/projects/2012/snow-fall/#/?part=tunnel-creek.
- go virtual. From your computer you can easily take a virtual tour of a college or stroll through a house you might want to purchase. Some new forms of nonfiction feel like pages ripped from a far-out science fiction novel. The USC Institute for Creative Technologies is bringing film- and game-industry artists together with computer and social scientists to study and develop "immersive media" for health therapies, science education, and even military training.

The world of nonfiction is rapidly becoming more visual, experiential, interactive, and multisensory. It may incorporate music, flash video, photographs, and animation. Course offerings at universities reflect the rapid transformation of this genre. Today the University of New Hampshire offers two different courses on "creative nonfiction."

But this renaissance in nonfiction has been slow to permeate elementary and secondary classrooms. In many schools we find kids still producing the same paint-by-number reports that I did when I was in school. And while the Common Core State Standards (CCSS) have brought renewed interest in nonfiction, I'm not convinced that they're encouraging livelier writing in this genre. I would argue that the CCSS have had the opposite impact.

We need to prepare students for the universe of today's nonfiction and the expectations that come with it. We need to open up their eyes to the wide range of possibilities available to any and all who want to communicate their expertise to the world. And we need to develop their critical literacy skills, so they are savvier consumers of media.

This book started with a tantalizing question: what would it look like for kids to create authentic nonfiction without relying on a formula, rubric, or rigid outline? What would it be like for students to make nonfiction from scratch? In the pages that follow we'll explore this idea. The book contains two parts: "Setting the Table: Tools of the Nonfiction Trade" and "Making Nonfiction in the Classroom." "Setting the Table" explores essential conditions, attitudes, and dispositions for making strong nonfiction. "Making Nonfiction in the Classroom" gets down to the nuts and bolts, looking at specific strategies and classroom structures we can use to help students find success in this genre. In an effort to make this book as practical as possible, I've also included "Classroom Connection" sections in some chapters to suggest immediate ways a teacher might put these ideas to use.

Any informational writing brings high expectations, as well it should. It must be accurate, insightful, and well organized, but it doesn't have to be deadly. Let's make our classrooms a place where students can create delicious nonfiction writing replete with passion, insight, and voice.

Part 1

SETTING THE TABLE: TOOLS OF THE NONFICTION TRADE

Chapter 1

STONE SOUP: A PARABLE

L ong ago, in a far-off land, a man and woman sat by the side of a road. They looked sweaty, dirty, and very tired indeed.

"I'm starved!" Mr. Nonfiction said. "I could eat a horse. I mean, not literally, but—"

"I know what you mean," Mrs. Nonfiction said wearily.

For several moments neither one of them spoke. Suddenly the man sat up and snapped his fingers.

"Say, I've got an idea. What we need is some soul food . . . something that will stick to your ribs. Whaddya say I make us a batch of stone soup?"

Mrs. Nonfiction looked doubtful. "Stone soup? Are you sure you know how to make it?"

"It's a cinch," Mr. Nonfiction assured his wife. "I've made it plenty of times before. One time I bought a can of it, which was a huge mistake. The stuff tasted awful! Nope, we're going to make stone soup the old-fashioned way. We're going to make it from scratch! Are you with me?"

Mrs. Nonfiction still didn't look convinced.

"Do you have a better idea?" he asked.

"No," she admitted.

So they set to work. While he began to build a fire, she took out a large pot and filled it with water.

"Do you have the stone?" she asked.

"I sure do. And what a magical stone it is!" Mr. Nonfiction produced a piece of cloth, which he carefully unfolded to reveal a rock, small and round. He lifted the stone and brought it to his eyes so he could study it. Then he ceremoniously dropped the stone into the pot of water. They heard it clunk against the bottom of the pot.

"That's all there is to it." As Mr. Nonfiction stirred the water he smacked his lips. "Mmm, this is going to be good!"

His wife still looked skeptical. "Looks pretty watery to me. Where's the flavor going to come from?"

Mr. Nonfiction laughed. "From the stone, my dear! The stone is a rock. There are three kinds of rocks: sedimentary, metamorphic, and igneous. That stone looks like a piece of granite, so it has to be—"

"Shh!" she hissed. "I hear someone coming!"

Sure enough, they saw a figure approaching.

"Halt!" Mr. Nonfiction cried. "Identify yourself!"

"It's just me: Poetry." It was a man wearing a long black robe. Moving closer, he peered into the pot. "What are you making?"

"Stone soup," Mr. Nonfiction told him. "It's a little . . . thin right now but it'll taste delicious when we finish." He grinned. "Hey, I made a rhyme! I'm a poet, and I didn't even know it!"

Poetry smiled. "You're a natural. You know, I've got a few ingredients with me. If you want, you can have them for your soup."

"What exactly do you have?"

"Just a few similes and metaphors," Poetry replied. "I thought they might make your soup taste better, you know, sweeten the broth."

Mr. Nonfiction frowned. "It's not really necessary."

"Of course not," Poetry agreed, "but it can't hurt, can it?"

Mr. Nonfiction looked at his wife.

She shrugged. "It's okay with me. This soup definitely needs *something*."

So Mr. Nonfiction reluctantly let Poetry throw his ingredients into the pot. Soon after Poetry left, a savory new smell began to waft into the air. A few minutes later they heard twigs snapping.

"Halt!" Mr. Nonfiction cried. This time he drew his sword from its sheath. "Who goes there?"

A bearded man appeared, his hair covered by a red scarf.

"It's just me: Comedy," the man said, holding up his hands. "Easy, mate, I don't mean any harm. Say, that's quite a sword you've got there."

"Yes, the blade is made of tempered steel," Mr. Nonfiction explained. "Tempering is a special treatment involving high heat. It makes the steel tougher by decreasing its hardness."

"Is that a fact?" Comedy asked.

"Yes," Mr. Nonfiction said solemnly. "It is a fact."

Comedy burst out laughing. The Nonfictions looked at each other, confused.

"What's so funny?"

"You guys are hysterical!" Comedy exclaimed. "Say, is that stone soup you're making? You know, I happen to have some extra humor with me . . . a few jokes, plus one story that's simply hilarious. It's quite fresh—I just picked it an hour ago. I thought you might like to add it to your soup."

Mr. Nonfiction hesitated. "Stone soup doesn't need any ingredients other than this magical stone itself."

"No, no, of course not," Comedy said quickly. "But I find that sometimes a dash of humor helps to bring out the flavor."

"Oh, all right," Mr. Nonfiction grumbled.

So the humor got stirred into the soup and Comedy waved good-bye, laughing as he went.

Soon another visitor appeared. She was a tall woman wearing a cloak and a large, black hat.

"Who are you?" Mr. Nonfiction demanded.

"Mystery," she replied. "Is that stone soup you're making? Say, I brought something to make your soup taste even better."

She held up a small package.

"What is it?" Mrs. Nonfiction asked.

Mystery flashed an inscrutable smile. "I can't tell you. It's a secret ingredient. But I promise you this: it will make your soup taste delicious."

Mr. Nonfiction glanced at his wife, exasperated. "I object. I mean, she won't even tell us what it is!"

Mrs. Nonfiction nodded. "Yes. But something tells me we should accept her gift."

After a moment's hesitation, Mr. Nonfiction took the package from Mystery and stirred the secret ingredients into the soup.

Mystery left. Their next visitor was a man with a large, round belly.

"What's going on here?" he cried in a booming voice. "Rumor has it that you're making stone soup!"

"Wow," Mrs. Nonfiction muttered. "News sure travels fast around here."

Mr. Nonfiction eyed the fat man suspiciously. "So what if we are? Who are you anyway?"

"I'm Story," the man explained. "You simply cannot make a suitable soup if you leave out my ingredients! Here, let me show you . . . I've got all kinds of goodies."

He began to pull things out of his pockets: anecdote, character, and setting. He started to throw them into the pot, but Mr. Nonfiction stopped his arm.

"Wait!" he protested. "Have you ever heard the expression 'Too many chefs spoil the broth'?"

Story smiled. "Tell you what. I'll make you a deal, okay? If these ingredients don't make your soup taste better, I'll . . . I'll . . ."

"You'll what?" Mr. Nonfiction demanded.

"I'll write you into an epic trilogy," Story promised. "I'll make you the hero."

Slyly Mr. Nonfiction raised his eyebrows. "A hero? With a beautiful princess?"

Story grinned. "More beautiful than you can imagine."

"Don't make her *too* beautiful," Mrs. Nonfiction warned.

"Okay, we'll compromise," her husband said. "Moderately beautiful."

"Whatever," Mrs. Nonfiction agreed.

And Story's ingredients got stirred into the soup.

"Oh, wait, I almost forgot!" Story cried. He pulled out a vial of what looked like greenish goop.

"What is that?" Mrs. Nonfiction cried in horror.

"Voice," Story replied. "That's the most crucial ingredient of all."

"I doubt that," Mr. Nonfiction grumbled, but he reluctantly allowed voice to be added to the soup.

After Story left, Mr. and Mrs. Nonfiction took turns stirring the liquid in the big pot. With the addition of all the new ingredients the steaming concoction became darker and thicker. It smelled delicious.

"It's starting to boil," Mr. Nonfiction observed. "Water boils at 212 degrees. But at high altitudes, the boiling point gets higher. That's because when the atmospheric pressure decreases—"

"BE QUIET!" his wife snapped.

Mr. Nonfiction looked stunned. "What's wrong? I thought facts were important to you."

"Right now I couldn't care less about the boiling point of water!" she hissed. "All I care about is getting some food into my belly!"

"I was just trying to be helpful," he said meekly.

"You're right, I'm sorry," she replied. "I get grumpy when I'm this hungry."

THAT'S a fact, he thought, but knew enough to keep it to himself.

Finally, the soup was ready. They ladled the rich broth into their bowls and began to eat. For a long moment they remained quiet, savoring the soup.

"What do you think?" Mr. Nonfiction asked. "Tasty, huh?"

"Mmmmm." She purred with pleasure. "Truly succulent."

They finished their soup and promptly helped themselves to a second helping, and a third. Finally they were sated. Mr. Nonfiction ceremoniously fished the rounded stone from the pot. He lifted it up and studied it closely.

"It takes a very special stone to make a soup this delicious," Mr. Nonfiction declared solemnly. He rinsed off the stone, dried it, wrapped it in cloth, and carefully stowed it away for another day.

In writing classrooms we spend a great deal of time making sure that our students understand distinctions between genres. This makes sense; certainly it's important that they know the conventions of various genres, how one kind of writing looks and feels different from another. But we do our students a disservice if we stop there and show them only the distinctions between genres. It's equally important that we show them the *commonalities* as well.

The Stone Soup parable may have a whimsical tone, but my message is deadly serious: skilled nonfiction writers enrich their work by drawing on strategies, techniques, and craft elements found in every other genre. Without those elements nonfiction would be thin gruel indeed, something few readers would find appetizing. Let's look briefly at some essential elements of nonfiction writing.

A Bold Lead

The lead may represent only 5 to 10 percent of the actual piece, but the nonfiction writer spends much more time crafting the lead because it's crucial to hooking the reader. It doesn't matter how strong the rest of the article is if nobody chooses to read it.

The lead establishes the voice and tone. At the same time it must quickly bring the reader into the subject matter. It has to be intriguing enough that the reader thinks, *Hmmm, I should read this.* All of this must be accomplished very quickly, usually within a few sentences, because fickle readers will jump to something more interesting if you don't hook them (Portalupi and Fletcher 2001).

Look at the lead Alan Weisman crafted for this article he wrote for CNN.

Why the Earth Is Farting

Every day, you have a close personal encounter with methane, a key ingredient of something we don't usually mention in polite company: farts. Perhaps that's why methane is also called "natural gas." Unfortunately, neither propriety nor intestinal discipline can suppress its unpleasantness lately, because now not just us, but the Earth itself is farting. (2014)

The article is about a sobering topic: the thawing and exploding of methane stored in the earth's crust. I'm concerned about the impact of global warming, but even so I might tend to skip an article on such a wonky subject. Weisman writes about a serious topic in a playful

Figure 1.1 Classroom Connection
Collecting Strong Nonfiction Leads

You'll want to spend time with your students studying exemplary nonfiction writing (see Chapter 6). Challenge your students to look for strong leads in nonfiction they find. What technique did the author use to grab the reader? A startling fact, quote, joke, or story? Use a flipchart or whiteboard to keep track of what they find.

manner. He uses a comparison we can all relate to. His striking lead pulls me in and compels me to read the whole thing. (See Figure 1.1.)

You can entice the reader with leads or with any of the other elements mentioned in this chapter: arresting detail, characterization, precise description, suspense, or similes and metaphors. Demonstrating these various techniques will attune students to what skilled nonfiction writers do and motivate them to incorporate a wider range of writing strategies/techniques into their nonfiction writing.

Convincing Characterization

I would name *place, plot,* and *character* as the three main components of a story. (You might add *mood* to that list.) But these aren't essential only to fiction; I'd argue that these elements are equally important in nonfiction, especially character. Look at this piece about Robert Kennedy and Jimmy Hoffa.

> *Martin, who was profiling the (Robert) Kennedy-Hoffa feud for the* Saturday Evening Post, *was driving with Kennedy down Capitol Hill on the way home one night when Kennedy noticed the lights still burned at the Teamster headquarters. Never to be outworked, Kennedy turned the car around and went back to his office. Hearing of Kennedy's reaction, Hoffa saw an opportunity for more winking mischief. He began leaving the lights turned on in his office after he went home at night.* (Thomas 2002, 81)

Evan Thomas uses this revealing anecdote to give us a deeper understanding of the drive and obsessive nature of these two men. We see a classic structure widely used in fiction—protagonist versus antagonist—and the tension/conflict/drama that ensues when one struggles with the other.

Arresting Detail

Students may be able to cite facts about Abraham Lincoln, but some of the most interesting ones are rarely mentioned. For instance, President Lincoln had an extremely close relationship with his sons. The death of his third son, Willie, at the age of eleven was a heavy blow to Lincoln. He was so distraught that he had the boy's body exhumed, twice, so he could look at his son's face.

Telling details like that give the nonfiction writer another great way of revealing character. Savvy nonfiction writers know that one or two unforgettable details like this are far more effective than a dozen bland ones. This detail—both gruesome and oddly tender—made an indelible impression on me when I first read it and gave me a window into the human side of this iconic president.

Precise Description

One of the major challenges nonfiction writers face is how to explain technical concepts and terms in a way that the average nonexpert might understand. In the following passage, Sebastian Junger explains *buoyancy*, something that's critically important in the nautical world:

> *Two forces are locked in combat for a ship like that: the downward push of gravity and the upward lift of buoyancy. Gravity is the combined weight of the vessel and everything on it—crew, cargo, fishing gear—seeking the center of the earth. Buoyancy is the force of all the enclosed air in the hull trying to rise above water level.*
>
> *Every boat has a degree of roll from which she can no longer recover. The* Queen Mary *came within a degree or two of capsizing off Newfoundland when a rogue wave burst her pilothouse windows ninety feet up; she sagged on her beam ends for an agonizing minute before regaining her trim.* (2009, 78)

When I write nonfiction I follow this rule: the more complicated the subject, the simpler the language I use. Junger certainly does that here. His writing is clear and straightforward. These two paragraphs give us a solid grasp of the subject. His decision to include this anecdote about the *Queen Mary* prevents this from being too abstract and dry, reminding us that in matters of buoyancy people's lives are at stake.

The best descriptions of technical data are done so well, you can't tell to which genre they belong. For instance, consider this description of the beam used in an Australian lighthouse during the 1920s.

> *The actual luminescence comes from a flame of vaporized oil that burns in an incandescent mantle. It gets magnified and directed through a giant set of glass prisms twelve feet high, called a first order Fresnel lens, which bends the light into a beam so intense you can see it more than thirty miles away.* (Stedman 2012, 188–189)

This passage uses a specialized vocabulary and careful explanation of a technical process; it has the sound and feel of nonfiction. In fact these sentences appear in *The Light Between Oceans*, a historical novel written by M. L. Stedman.

Suspense/Foreshadowing

As with any compelling story, a strong piece of nonfiction is fueled by tension and suspense—the sense that something is about to happen. Skilled nonfiction writers often create that suspense early in the piece to hook the reader. This is the first paragraph describing Hurricane Floyd:

> *In one city after another, the streets fell silent. Jacksonville, Florida. Charleston, South Carolina. Wilmington, North Carolina. These usually bustling cities became ghost towns under gray skies. Empty homes with boarded up windows lined silent, rain-drenched streets. Miles of cars snaked slowly away, looking for higher ground and shelter.* (*TIME for Kids* 1999)

Once again, we have a nonfiction writer employing the tools of a fiction writer. If you didn't know it, you might think this is the beginning of a novel instead of a *TIME for Kids* article. The details have been carefully chosen to communicate the sense of danger and impending doom.

Metaphors and Similes

One of the best ways to explain a complex idea is to compare it to something close to the reader's experience. Consider this piece about black holes, "It's Snack Time in the Cosmos," published in the *New York Times*.

> *Now, for the first time, astronomers may have a chance to watch as a giant black hole consumes a cosmic snack.*
>
> *In March or April, a gas cloud that has been hurtling toward the center of the Milky Way is expected to collide with Sagittarius A, a black hole that lies just 26,000 light-years from Earth. (The actual event, of course, took place 26,000 years ago.) The cloud is as massive as three Earths—no match for the black hole, which has the mass of four million suns.*

*"This is a rare opportunity to witness spoon-feeding of a black hole,"
said Avi Loeb, a theoretical astrophysicist at Harvard. "Will the gas
reach the black hole, and if so, how quickly? Will the black hole throw
up or spit the gas out in the form of an outflow or a jet?*

*"The experience is as exciting for astronomers," he went on, "as it is
for parents taking the first photos of their infant eating."* (Cowen 2014)

Like Weisman in his piece about exploding methane, Ron Cowen
uses a comparison (feeding a baby) that we can all relate to. By doing
so, Cowen helps make this subject approachable to everyday readers.

For a long time I've had the nagging feeling that too many young writers are "compartmentalized thinkers." Perhaps we're partly to blame
by teaching craft elements as if they are specific to one genre only.
That's a mistake.

"Remember that the craft of writing, what writers know how to do
with words and sentences and the organization of ideas, is something
that *crosses* genres," Katie Wood Ray reminds us in her book *Study
Driven.* "The writer of a memoir published in a picture book intended
for children might choose and place words in exactly the same way a
writer crafting an essay for the back page of *Time* magazine chooses
and places words . . . Because craft crosses genre, finding texts rich
with craft-teaching potential is critical because the teaching has no
boundaries. In other words, what students learn about writing well
in one genre can help them write well in many other genres" (2006,
101–102).

Certainly our students need to be aware of the unique properties of
the nonfiction genre. But perhaps we might encourage them to think
less "nonfiction" and more "strong writing" when they craft their
informational writing. When our students make nonfiction, we need
to keep reminding them: You have to bring it all when you write. Don't
hold anything back. Bring everything you know as a writer about how
to animate your material and make it come alive for the reader.

Chapter 2

LESSONS FROM WORKING AS
A FREELANCE WRITER

I spent a dozen years writing feature articles for the *Wall Street Journal, People, Cosmopolitan,* and various in-flight magazines. In some ways I'm still living that life. After I get a tentative idea for a book—say, about the struggles of boy writers—I incubate it in my writer's notebook. If it seems sufficiently promising I start developing the concept, gathering, talking to people, doing some preliminary research. In time I might propose it to one of my editors and, eventually, start working on a book or article. In this chapter I'm going to share a few lessons I've gleaned from working as a freelance writer and try to build a bridge from my experience to the nonfiction writing that takes place in our classrooms.

Finding Material to Write About

I started working as a freelancer after graduating from college. I had moved back to my parents' home in West Islip, a commuter town on the south shore of Long Island, New York. Early each morning hundreds of women and men (my father among them) headed to the train station and rode the Long Island Railroad (LIRR) into New York City. At first blush it didn't strike me as a promising place to find exciting material for a feature article. The real action, I knew, could be found an hour away in Manhattan.

If you're a writer on a magazine staff you have the luxury of a regular paycheck, plus a senior editor who tells you what to write about. As a freelance writer, I had neither. It would be up to me to unearth something important or intriguing to write about. But what?

I started by doing what I always do, casting a wide net, looking for possible ideas. I talked to my friends, my friends' parents, my parents' friends, relatives, former teachers. It didn't take long to find a few promising possibilities.

- I ran into a former teacher who mentioned that Mario Puzo (author of *The Godfather*) lived in West Islip. It wasn't hard to find out where he lived and get his phone number. It took me several days to screw up my courage, but finally I called him at home and asked if he might let me interview him for a magazine profile. Puzo was extremely cordial. He told me he was intensely busy, but suggested I try him again later that year. I never did actually meet him; still, this iconic author was there and accessible.
- It turned out that we had a famous person living right on our street: Al Oerter, renowned discus thrower who won gold medals in four consecutive Olympics. I went to Oerter's house and knocked on his door. He was a bit shy at first, but when he realized I was a neighbor he graciously agreed to schedule an interview. Eventually I published two articles about him.
- Through a friend, I found out about Tanya Grosman, a lithographer who had a studio in West Islip that was named Limited Art Editions. Grosman had begun to lure world-class artists like Larry Rivers and Robert Rauschenberg to her studio to paint on stone and make lithographic prints. I contacted her, set up an interview, spent an entire day with her, and eventually published a feature about Grosman and her studio.

So I didn't have to go into Manhattan to find exciting material for a feature article. It turned out that there were plenty of stories in West Islip, a sleepy commuter town no different from the other two hundred small towns on Long Island. The stories were right under my nose! I just needed to dig to find them. (See Figure 2.1.)

Finding My Angle

Once at a cocktail party I met an editor for *Sports Illustrated*. I revered this magazine, so it took a great deal of courage for me to approach this editor and introduce myself.

Figure 2.1 Classroom Connection
Making an Expert List

Finding a topic can be a daunting challenge for students. We can defuse this issue by helping them tune in to and "read" the world around them. You might have your students survey people they know: parents, relatives, older siblings, teachers, or business owners. Students could put together a list of questions designed to ferret out what hidden knowledge and expertise these individuals might possess:

- What are your hobbies? Your passions?
- Have you ever had an unusual job?
- Have you ever lived in another country?
- Would you be willing to be interviewed about this subject or place?

A survey like this will help students become aware of the people who are insiders in various subjects. It will open up a range of possibilities for nonfiction topics. Not only that, but it will encourage students to learn through a personal connection (an interview) instead of merely pulling facts from books.

Ralph: I, uh, I have an idea for an article I'd like to write for your magazine.

Editor: About what?

Ralph: Baseball.

Editor (smiling): Baseball is a pretty broad subject. What would your angle be?

Ralph: Baseball pitchers.

Editor: Any pitchers in particular?

Ralph: I'd like to write a piece about baseball pitchers over forty who tried to come back after having Tommy John surgery.

Editor (nodding): I see. That might be intriguing . . .

I never did write a piece about baseball for *Sports Illustrated*; still, the conversation was instructive. The editor had an impromptu writing conference with me, a back-and-forth dialogue that helped me narrow my subject and find a workable slice of the pie. I have published enough nonfiction to know that taking too broad an approach often leads to bland, list writing. It's paramount that I get a workable focus or angle on what I'm writing about.

Although narrowing or altering my focus happens throughout the process, it often starts when I propose the idea in the first place. Writing a proposal letter is a crucial step—it gets both the editor and me thinking about focus and my audience. Some years ago I proposed an article to *Cosmopolitan* magazine about women who decide to get a tattoo (this was well before tattooing was all the rage). Helen Gurley Brown wrote back and said, "Yes, we would be interested, but we'd like you to focus on professional, white-collar women. That's the readership we're aiming for." That's the article I wrote.

Research

The organization of this chapter might give the misleading idea that finding a workable angle and researching my subject are two distinct processes. In fact, they are very much intertwined. My early research helps me focus my topic, but at the same time, figuring out my angle helps me realize what information I will need to dig up for the finished piece.

I think of my research as taking a crash course on my subject. This is a rather peculiar phrase—why a *crash* course? Yet there is a kind of violence or at least abruptness in the way a nonfiction writer must plunge headfirst into a subject. I cast a wide net as I try to cram/learn as much about my topic as I possibly can. I like to start with a blank new notebook when I'm researching. That way everything I learn—facts, stats, quotes, sketches, new words, a list of sources—can be collected in one place. There are certain basic assumptions that underlie my research:

- The world is a fascinating place. There's something interesting about almost any topic—it's my job to find it.
- I'm not as unique as I might imagine. In fact I'm very much like most other people, so whatever intrigues me will probably be

similar to what will intrigue my readers.

- Curiosity is strength. Nowadays this quality often gets described in pejorative terms—*she's nosy, a stalker, a creeper*—which is unfortunate. If nonfiction could be described as an engine, surely curiosity is its fuel. Cultivating an inquisitive attitude is helpful, even essential, for any who hope to write strong nonfiction. (For more on curiosity, see Chapter 4.)

Questions

"Live the questions," the German poet Rainer Maria Rilke wrote in *Letters to a Young Poet*, and I live by that credo. Questions feature prominently in my research process; in fact, I consider them to be more important than answers. Questions keep me grounded. I know that the questions I have will likely be the same questions my readers will have. And I've learned that during the course of my research my questions will change, starting off general in the beginning and becoming more sophisticated and detailed by the end.

For instance, when I was writing about tattooing, my initial questions reflected what I figured most readers would want to know. Is it painful to get a tattoo? Is it generally safe? Is it expensive? After I found answers to those basic questions (yes, yes, no) I could move on to more sophisticated questions about tattoo design. Later I would try to tease out interesting stories and reasons connected to why a person might choose to get a tattoo.

While I seek out many different types of resources, I've rarely found anything better than talking to a real person. I try hard to find somebody to interview, a person with expertise in whatever I'm writing about. And I need to learn about the people I'm going to interview ahead of time. Knowing their background and accomplishments prepares me so I can ask intelligent questions. This kind of "preresearch" is an important part of my process. After I do that I put together a list of interview questions. During the interview I try to get all my questions answered, but at the same time I know I'll also have to think on my feet and respond to what the interviewee says. It's important to stay flexible enough so I can ask follow-up questions if the person says something unexpected I might want to pursue.

Drafting

Putting together a piece of finished nonfiction happens quickly for me, often during the course of a single week, but a lot must happen during that time. Before I start writing I make a point of talking about my subject with a trusted friend. Talking helps me get more comfortable with what I'm writing about. And while I'm explaining my subject, I pay close attention to how my friend is reacting. Where does she seem interested, perplexed, bored? What other questions does she have? Her response will definitely help me shape and revise the article. (See Figure 2.2.)

The entire process of creating a piece happens over a period of time. I can't think of a time when I've written a nonfiction piece in one fell swoop. I always do a number of drafts, sharpening and ideally improving the piece with each successive draft. I like to revise early in the process, when the "clay" is still soft and I'm trying to figure out the shape of what I'm writing.

I've learned the hard way that I cannot be afraid to leave out some of the facts, stats, quotes, and other research I've dug up. In fact, what I leave out is every bit as important as what I include.

During the process of drafting I'm thinking "strong writing" as much as "nonfiction." I want to create the kind of piece that will seize readers' imaginations. I need to bring everything I know about vivid writing—precise description, arresting details, compelling metaphors, memorable quotes, and so on—to grab readers' attention and keep them engrossed right up to the end.

Figure 2.2 Classroom Connection
Talk Out Your Topic

Get your students into pairs or groups of three and invite them to talk about their nonfiction subjects before they try writing a first draft. This activity does incur a certain cost. It will raise the noise level in the class and eat up fifteen or twenty minutes of class time, but even so it's valuable.

When your students talk, their tendency will be to look down at their note cards containing facts and research they have gathered. This tendency will interrupt whatever flow and halting fluency they might have. It might be more worthwhile for them to talk without referring to any notes. The purpose here is more to build confidence than to receive a thorough critique, so keep things positive. Students in the listening role should be alert and as supportive as possible. Suggest that they offer one positive comment and one suggestion after their partner finishes talking about his or her subject.

Chapter 3

LOUISE BORDEN: TOOLS OF THE NONFICTION TRADE

L ouise Borden has published twenty-eight books for young readers, eight of which are nonfiction. Some of her popular titles are *Fly High! The Story of Bessie Coleman*; *The Little Ships: The Heroic Rescue at Dunkirk in World War II*; *The Journey That Saved Curious George: The True Wartime Escape of Margret and H. A. Rey*; and *Touching the Sky: The Flying Adventures of Wilbur and Orville Wright*. I asked a series of questions to get her to explain the process she goes through in creating nonfiction.

Ralph: Can you talk about the roots of your interest in nonfiction?

Louise: My friend Richard Peck states, "We write by the light of every book we've ever read . . ." So all the books I read and loved as a child, and the books I've read as an adult, shine a light across my shoulder when I go to my desk. I've always loved reading biographies, autobiographies, and nonfiction books about history that hold my attention.

My roots come from the biographies I read in elementary school. If any books of fiction contained epilogues, or authors' notes or maps, these drew me in as well. I don't have strong roots in science nonfiction, but more in books about artists, writers, photographers—people who inspire me—and important events in history. I majored in history in college so I have the experience (and stamina!) to read long nonfiction texts.

Ralph: I've been thinking about the habits of a good nonfiction writer: curiosity, passion, for instance. What do you consider important habits? Do you think that these habits can be nurtured?

Louise: To write nonfiction, a writer certainly needs curiosity and passion. I would add patience and perseverance, because each time I begin a nonfiction project I know I'll have to wade through dozens of reference books (some boring and dry) to gain a deeper understanding of my subject. Then my challenge is to find the right structure plus the essential, intriguing details that will inform but also engage my reader.

I had outstanding social studies teachers in elementary school. Every student in my classroom was an explorer. I believe that curiosity is fostered by terrific teaching. Realistically when kids write nonfiction in school they won't be as deeply immersed in their subject as I have to be when I'm writing a book. But if they love the subject (and get to choose their own), they won't mind the work of finding good information.

I took Henry, a kindergartner, to see *The Lemurs of Madagascar,* an IMAX movie. As soon as he got home he rushed to his desk and, on his own, created a small nonfiction book about lemurs. Passion and curiosity!

This same kid had checked a book out of the library about the Greeks and the Trojan horse. Henry wanted to write his own book about Ulysses, King Priam, Helen, and the wooden horse. We worked on the text together, and then he drew pictures for each page. He had a real interest in the subject. Teachers need to find ways to engage students so they can explore their own interests via nonfiction.

Ralph: Tell me a bit about the process you go through when creating a book. I'm interested in how you circle in and ultimately land on a particular idea. Do you keep lists or files of possible subjects?

Louise: I don't keep lists but I might put a few notes in a file and then bring out that file when I'm ready to embark on the research process.

Ralph: How can you tell if an idea is substantial enough, and has enough heft for a whole book?

Louise: Because I'm a student of history, I marvel at true stories and events. When something has emotional resonance for me, I know I'll someday try to write about it. Take, for example, my hero Raoul Wallenberg, the heroic little ships, the inventor John Harrison, Bessie Coleman's determination, Margret and H. A. Rey riding on bicycles in a sea of millions of refugees. Often I have to hang on to that hope, to that enduring image in my mind, for several years before I begin gathering research materials.

One of my mentors, William Zinsser, states, "Every successful piece of nonfiction should leave the reader with one provocative thought that he or she didn't have before . . . so decide what thought you want to leave in the reader's mind."

Zinsser also says, "People and places are the twin pillars on which most nonfiction is built." I think if I have true passion for a subject, and can make it accessible for a young reader, then it will have enough heft.

Ralph: Does it matter if somebody else has already written about a person or event?

Louise: No. There are many famous people, events, or interesting places I want to write about. The key is to write about them in a new way. For example, when Trish Marx and I wrote about the Wright brothers, we decided to focus not on Kitty Hawk and the 1903 flight but on Wilbur and Orville's historic flights in 1909. This came about because I saw a photograph of a canoe attached to Wilbur's flyer.

> One of my mentors, William Zinsser, states, "Every successful piece of nonfiction should leave the reader with one provocative thought that he or she didn't have before . . . so decide what thought you want to leave in the reader's mind."

My father owned a small plane when I was growing up, and I often flew with my dad. That's why I've written three books about aviation. Two are nonfiction, and one is historical fiction, grounded in research about Charles Lindbergh and a flight he took across Mississippi in 1929.

Ralph: So would you say that your history with your father planted the deep roots for your interest in Lindbergh?

Louise: Yes, my dad often took us flying . . . from Ohio to Michigan or from Denver to Ohio, or from Ohio to the Bahamas. I grew up with his love of small planes. This led me to admire early aviators like Amelia Earhart (whom I've not written about) and Charles Lindbergh. And I read all of Anne Lindbergh's books because she was a poet and writer. Much later, I would learn about Bessie Coleman and coauthor a book about her as well as the Wright brothers.

> The writer's job is to show readers that these times were lived in color—just as our lives are lived in color today.

During our research about the Wright brothers Trish and I were excited to discover that the Wright canoe still exists. It was stored in the rafters of a barn. I climbed up a narrow ladder to see the canoe and noticed a small plaque indicating the name of the boat store on Broadway in New York City where the canoe was purchased in September of 1909. Amazing!

At that time the canoe was red. Now it's green, as Orville had it repainted years later, after Wilbur's death. Peter Fiore, our illustrator, shows the plaque in the scene with the red canoe on the grass. In the black-and-white photo, notice the flag on Wilbur's flyer in the photo. Notice that Wilbur is wearing a coat and tie and hat. Notice the fragile struts of the flyer.

Ralph: It sounds like primary sources are an important part of your research.

Louise: Yes. When I research I look at lots of old black-and-white photographs. The writer's job is to show readers that these times were lived in color—just as our lives are lived in color today.

I knew the idea of writing about Margret and H. A. Rey's escape from Paris had heft, but could I find their story? Could I find the true details of their long-ago escape?

Writing about Raoul Wallenberg was daunting. I'm not an academic. But I noticed that in the fifty or so books for adults that have been published on R. W., none contain more than a dozen photos. I wanted to know what the places and people in Raoul Wallenberg's story looked like. I knew kids would as well. *His Name Was Raoul Wallenberg* contains over one hundred photos. I believe that we need the best, most interesting information to engage young readers. For that project I went to Sweden three times, and to Budapest twice.

Ralph: Do you use a writer's notebook?

Louise: Yes, I do have a writer's notebook. I carry one with me. I have dozens I've written in, and I have dozens of new ones I've collected over my travels. I'm very particular about my notebooks. They are usually lined or quadrille. I like large flat notebooks. And I like plain covers. These are working notebooks I use when I need to focus on my subjects: Dunkirk, or a skating race in Holland, or the Holocaust in Budapest or the French Resistance (my current project). I write in notebooks when I'm alone or traveling. I write about the places, people I meet, observations from the road. Sometimes I write poems about these places.

Ralph: Do you use a separate notebook for nonfiction?

Louise: Yes, I have separate notebooks where I gather information, facts, and notes about my progress. I carry these with me on travels, or to places like the Library of Congress. I have one notebook I've been carrying for three years so it's really worn . . . I need to have a new cover put on it!

Sometimes I use foldout notebooks to record a time line or chronology. (Moleskine makes a great little notebook with pages that unfold; they call it a Japanese notebook.) I took one of these to Budapest when I attended a symposium on Raoul Wallenberg during my research, and used it just to take notes and make small travel sketches. The notebook in this photo of my desk is a chronology of events I want to narrate in a new nonfiction project.

Ralph: Could you give some insight into your research process?

Louise (smiling): On my sixth-grade report card, my teacher, Mrs. Resor, wrote, "I think that Louise will always enjoy research. Bon voyage!" I wonder how she knew?

I usually begin by gathering books, photos, and any information about that subject. I put all of these into several big boxes. If I'm still working on another book, these boxes are on the back burner of my writing stove. Then, when I have several free months ahead of me, I begin.

I start by thinking about what I already know and what more I need to learn. I wonder, Will I have to go to a city or another country? Whom might I talk to who knows a lot about this subject?

Ralph: So you actually start listing questions?

Louise: I don't make a list of questions but I write notes along with questions on a big sheet of paper or on a notebook page. At first they are scattered randomly across the page. Or I may make a web. Then later I might make a list that looks like this:

> Check the Library of Congress map division.
>
> Email the British Library.

And I start writing down names of people I want to contact, who I think might have firsthand information about my subject. I always interview lots of people.

I love maps and photos. These may not appear in my book but I study them again and again to get the details into my words.

Then I study those primary sources you mentioned. I read and reread first-person accounts. I look at old newspapers. I look at films about the time period or the subject. I immerse myself totally in what I'm studying and writing about.

I'm familiar with World War II and have a huge library of books about this time period. When I have questions, I write them in my research notebook and then try to gather the answers. As I gather letters and information, I put these in folders—place, person, etc.—to keep them organized.

Ralph: What have you learned about interviewing people?

Louise: I've learned to listen more than ask questions. As the interviewer, your job is to listen. It's important to let the other person speak, ramble, and recount. A few times I taped the interview, but I don't anymore. I begin with some key questions and then just listen and take notes.

Also, do your homework ahead of time, and think about what you want to learn. What is it that you don't yet know that you need to find out? Sometimes an interview will give you rich details about things you already know about. Those details are essential to crafting good writing.

Ralph: So many kids don't narrow their topics to a manageable size when they try to write nonfiction. Do you have any advice for teachers whose students tend to bite off more than they can chew?

Louise: I often have the same problem! The rescue at Dunkirk was huge and complicated. Even so, it was a small event in the vast canvas of World War II. To narrow the focus, I chose to use historical fiction. I tried to write a story in thirty-two pages with a character from my imagination and set her against the backdrop of a true event that has inspired me since college.

Making a time line can be very helpful when you're writing nonfiction. I do this early in my process. It's something students could do to see the important parts of the subject they could focus on.

Ralph: Do you think about what angle/focus you want to take with your subject? Is that part of your revision process?

Louise: The angle or focus for me comes earlier than the revision stage. I think about the structure of the text before I begin writing. Will the text be divided into parts (*Fly High!*) or will it read as a continuous narrative (*Sea Clocks*)? Will the reader need clues (maps, dates on a page as part of the design of the book) along the way?

Ralph: Do your editors ever suggest that you need to change or narrow the focus?

Louise: Yes, sometimes they do. They may point out that I'm trying to convey two subjects at the same time. Or they may suggest in a fictional book that I have too much going on in the story and to focus more on the character, etc. Usually I'm satisfied with the structure I've decided on earlier. But even that could change during the revision process if I realize that I've chosen the wrong one.

Ralph: When you research, what kind of information or factual nuggets are you looking for?

Louise: I'm looking for fascinating details: the American flag on Wilbur's flyer, the tiny pocket calendar that H. A. Rey carried during his escape, etc. I'm looking for how I can create a strong setting (Stockholm and Budapest in *His Name Was Raoul Wallenberg*). I'm looking for ways to engage my readers rather than bore them. An archival image such as a passport picture of Raoul as a boy is compelling proof and evidence. Then I surround myself with these bits of factual gold as I am writing the text.

Ralph: You actually went to Dunkirk in order to write *The Little Ships.* How does visiting a historical place inspire you?

Louise: The English novelist Frederick Forsyth said that there's no substitute for going to a place to create an authentic setting. I DID go to the beaches of Dunkirk, but I should point out that I'd already written most of the text. I was able, through photos and first-person accounts, to create that setting at my desk in Cincinnati. I changed very little after seeing the actual place. I've crossed the English Channel several times with the original little ships. And when I do, I feel as if I'm living part of my book.

In *The Journey That Saved Curious George* I was able to go to the Terrass Hotel in Paris, and also find the Château du Feuga in the south of France. I felt like a detective, a pathfinder. It was incredibly moving to drive up that gravel driveway to the château and know that I was the first person in over sixty years to try to track the Reys' story.

Setting is VERY important in nonfiction writing. Kids can use their eyes and ears to write about familiar settings or places close to home. A baseball stadium. Their school playground. A pond. For places farther afield, they can be armchair travelers/ researchers via the web.

Ralph: What happens when you search but can't find some information you consider important for your book?

Louise: I have to decide how important it is. In *The Journey That Saved Curious George* I didn't know the name of the ship that carried the Reys from Rio to New York City in October of 1940.

I decided it was okay for the reader not to know the actual ship's name for the final scene when the Reys arrive in New York Harbor.

But after the book was published I still was curious enough to pursue the name of that second ship. By that time Google was in full force. So I tracked the ship name from knowing that in 1940, the *New York Times* always published the names of ships arriving in port each day. By matching the October 14 date to ships coming from South America, I was able to find that the Reys arrived on the *Uruguay*. What a thrill to see their names on the ship's manifest. (Thank you, Ancestry.com!)

Ralph: That's wonderful! Would you consider adding this detail in a new edition of this book?

Louise: Well, it might be hard to squeeze in to the body of the text with an already set design but perhaps I might include it in the author's note if there's space.

If narrative nonfiction doesn't have a strong voice, it will not engage either the young reader or the adult reader.

Ralph: Can you give me a sense of how you revise your nonfiction books?

Louise: Sometimes when I get to one of my final drafts (final in that I think I'm almost there), I'll line up the pages across the floor. This helps me see the pacing of the book.

I always read my pages aloud. Always. This helps me to remove words that slow the narrative or possibly trip up the reader. I pay close attention to the voice of the text. Voice is very important to me. If narrative nonfiction doesn't have a strong voice, it will not engage either the young reader or the adult reader.

Sometimes during this part of the process I write notes to myself about facts I want to double-check—a date, or the spelling of a name (Hungarian!). Then I'll go find that page and make corrections. I print out the text, carry it with me on travels, revise with my pen, and then type in the changes and then print out the draft and read it again, make changes, etc. It's a process that seems to work but sometimes then I worry if I've overwritten the text.

Revision for me involves writing and rewriting those words countless times. This process includes

> reading the words aloud for the voice.
>
> deleting a word or two.
>
> adding a phrase.
>
> deleting a whole section.
>
> moving sentences around.
>
> rereading it aloud.

Writing is all about making choices. But true revision makes the work so much stronger. It's a part of the process that I enjoy because I know it will lead to a better book.

Ralph: I've heard you say that you create a dummy (a mock-up of the book) as part of your process.

Louise: Yes, I make dummies for all my books. I even made one for the 144-page book about Raoul Wallenberg. I need to turn the pages of the dummy to see how the book reads.

Ralph: My illustrators have made the dummies for my picture books. Interesting that you, as the writer, create the dummies. Do you sketch the illustrations or use preliminary sketches from the illustrator?

Louise: These dummies are solely for me as the writer as I try to find just the right words. I do this long before I even send the manuscript to an editor. There are no illustrations or sketches but I may place photos on various pages that I can later show to my editor if the book is going to be illustrated with photos.

I might make several dummies or just use one and keep taping revised text into it. I know my picture books will be illustrated by an artist and my job is the text. So my dummy only has text but it helps me envision the book page by page, spread by spread. I find it helpful to see the words and white space on the page, and see the pacing of the narrative. Later, an illustrator will get typed pages of text (not my dummy) and make his or her own dummy with sketches to work on with the publisher's art director/ designer.

Ralph: *The Little Ships* is written through the eyes of a teenage girl and narrated by her. So it would seem to me that you had a dual challenge: you had to include the relevant information and at the same time you had to stay true to her voice and her character. Can you comment on that?

Louise: This is one of my favorite books because it's told in a strong voice. I enjoy writing in first person more than third person. I think I'm a better writer in first person. I feel as if I become the character when I write in first person.

I've spent all my summers in northern Michigan—in boats and on water. So I had that background and that interest in a maritime setting. I write in a poetic style, so I have to keep only the most essential details in the lines. But I'm informing the reader in each line about what is happening in history.

I love the revision stage because the work has been done: gathering and writing down the information. Now I just need to streamline the story and make it seamless and beautiful but still accessible to young readers. This is my constant challenge.

I chose to write *The Little Ships* as historical fiction rather than nonfiction so I could draw the reader into the time and the place using a girl as the narrator. I used a first person voice in two other historical fiction texts: *The Greatest Skating Race* and *Sleds on Boston Common.* The endnotes for these three books are third person nonfiction. I like to include interesting information but I don't like long endnotes in books.

Ralph: Why not?

Louise: Some nonfiction books these days have simple text, and then they end with two or three pages of dense paragraphs of additional facts about the subject. These endnotes are not for kids, they're for adults. Few young readers will care about or read all that information.

I'm always conscious of what engages kids, and I hope they understand, and are inspired by, the subjects I've tried to share when they get to the end of my nonfiction books. I want kids to be able to read and enjoy any endnote that I include.

Ralph: What principles guide you as a nonfiction writer?

Louise: Less is more. I choose each word with care and that comes through finding words that match pictures in my head, and by endless paring down and revision. My early drafts are longer and crammed with information in clunky phrases.

Ralph: So, in subsequent drafts, you try to make the text flow more naturally?

Louise: Yes. With the fewest words possible.

Ralph: How do you "un-clunk" your sentences?

Louise: I remove adverbs, and any line or phrase that is repetitive of an image I am trying to convey in the text. I remove generic words and strive for specific details. I remove small words like *always, all, just, then*. Each word has to earn its place in the story. Each sentence should lead the reader into the next.

Chapter 4

HELPFUL ATTITUDES FOR MAKING NONFICTION

Education is not the filling of a pail but the lighting of a fire.

—W. B. Yeats

Making nonfiction can be a long and arduous process for any writer. Certain provisions—attitudes or dispositions—are helpful for completing this journey. These would include the following.

Curiosity

Everyone in my family knows that I'm mesmerized by spiders. Some years back we rented a vacation home. Soon after we arrived my kids came flying into the house.

"What is it?" my wife, JoAnn, asked, but my kids wanted to talk to me.

"Dad, there's a giant spider outside!"

My kids discovered long ago that I was (am) a spider freak, and had no doubt that I'd be eager and excited to see a large tropical arachnid, as indeed I was. They knew that I'd be fascinated by every detail: its coloring, fangs, the web structure, remnants of insects it had eaten, and so on.

At first blush it would seem that certain subjects pique our curiosity while others do not. Although this can be true, curiosity is not always an on/off toggle switch. Sometimes this feeling grows slowly over time.

I realized this while interviewing Diane Ackerman, one of my favorite nonfiction writers and the author of *A Natural History of the Senses* and *One Hundred Names for Love.*

"I tend to be quietly thinking about a subject for a while," she told me, "and become more fascinated by it over time before I settle down to actually writing a book about it."

This has implications for the nonfiction classroom. We should encourage students to let their curiosity evolve, and remind them not to limit themselves to the same old subjects they have tended to research in the past.

It's important to share our own curiosity in the classroom, though I would strike a note of caution. Kids have a finely tuned detector for fake passion and enthusiasm (such as when we pretend to get excited about an upcoming test). Modeling false curiosity does more harm than good. We're most genuine when we share our curiosity about a subject in which we're truly interested. When Carl Anderson taught middle school he would frequently make references to the Beatles, so his students were well aware of his fascination (obsession?) with the Fab Four. Some went so far as to parody Carl's obsession in their own writing. One student wrote a hilarious piece in which John Lennon taught Paul McCartney how to take a song through the "writing process."

"Curiosity urges you on—the driving force," wrote author John Dos Passos. Tapping into kids' curiosity is crucial to helping them develop the stamina to write nonfiction that is lively and accurate. We should recognize and affirm this quality when we see it in our students, though in today's rigid educational climate curiosity can sometimes be problematic.

Case in point: One afternoon three third-grade boys in a school in Washington State found a six-inch lizard on the playground. The boys brought it inside, excited and eager to learn more about it. This put the teacher in a dilemma.

"It felt like a fork in the road," she told me. "There was no place in my plan book for an impromptu lizard study. We were doing a mini-unit on test preparation—the lizard thing felt like a major distraction. But the kids' questions were so great. What species was it? What was it doing in the playground? Could it have laid eggs? Might it have been following a path in search of water? They really wanted to know! So

I told the students we could put the test prep unit on hold for a little while, and try to learn everything we could about that lizard. It turned out to be the best thing we did all year."

Teachable moments like that are rich, rare, and unanticipated. This raises an important question: how can we revise our classrooms to make them flexible enough so we can recognize a moment for curiosity-fueled inquiry and jump on it?

Grit and Persistence

I recently attended an educational conference where the buzz was all about "grit." Several speakers quoted Angela Lee Duckworth, a psychologist at the University of Pennsylvania, who identifies *grit* as the most important factor in predicting success. Duckworth defines *grit* as "Passion and perseverance for a long-term goal . . . Grit is having stamina . . . it's living life like it's a marathon, not a sprint."

Grit and perseverance are certainly important qualities to have when researching nonfiction. Nonfiction subjects are akin to pistachio nuts—some break apart easily, while others are much more difficult to crack open.

How can we help students develop the grit and the stamina to hang in there as they research their topics? Anecdotal evidence would suggest that kids get frustrated and lose heart when the going gets tough. Yet students certainly do demonstrate grit and persistence in other parts of their lives—sports, for instance. Author Kelly Milner Halls taps into the world of video games when she challenges students to dig deeper with their topics (see Figure 4.1).

Figure 4.1 Classroom Connection
Helping Young Nonfiction Writers Build Stamina

Kelly Milner Halls has written a number of high-interest nonfiction books for young readers, including *In Search of Sasquatch, Alien Investigation: Searching for the Truth About*

UFOs and Aliens, and *Tales of the Cryptids: Mysterious Creatures That May or May Not Exist.* I asked Kelly about how we might help students persevere in their nonfiction research. Here is her response.

When I talk to kids about research I compare it to playing video games. This is a great way to make sure that my boys are ENGAGED. Here's how I present this idea during one of the many author visits I make to schools. After defining albinism *for my students I might share a photograph of an albino axolotl salamander (from my book* Albino Animals*). I ask if there are any (video) gamers in the crowd, and of course there are dozens. I admit my house is a gaming household, too.*

"Do you quit a game after the first level?" I ask the students.

"No way!" the kids (usually boys) yell out.

"You might get frustrated, throw the controller across the room, and go outside to play ball for a while," I continue. "But you always come back and finish the level. Am I right?"

The kids laugh and agree.

"Do you quit at the end of the second level?"

"No!"

"The third? Okay. Do you usually stay with it long enough to beat the game?"

"Yeah."

"Well, research is exactly like a video game," I tell the students. "At the first level of that game, you discover an albino salamander with his own website. Cool, but so what? At the second level, you discover that if you cut off its leg the leg grows back. That's pretty neat, but so does a starfish. If you beat the third level, you discover that if you crush vertebrae in its backbone, the salamander's body will repair it. If you play through the next level, you discover another amazing thing. Cut away a slice of this animal's brain, and its body will replace that, too."

By now the kids are spellbound.

"Wanna beat the game?" I ask.

"Yeah!"

Kids respond to this with puzzled looks.

"Let's say you're making a salad for your mother, chopping lettuce," I continue. "You're not paying attention and you chop your pinky finger off! You want to rush the piece to the doctor so he can sew it back on, but it falls on the floor where your dog is waiting. He eats it. Dang, I hate when that happens!"

Kids burst out laughing.

Now I stick out my pinky finger, wiggle it, and ask, "Would you like to know how to grow a new one? If they can figure out how the salamander regenerates his body parts, is it possible we could teach OUR bodies how to do it too?"

A Taste for Complex Truths

The nonfiction writer is trying to put together a story. But every story has two (or more) sides. The writer knows she may dig up certain information that challenges, complicates, or even trumps other facts.

- Naturalists are heartened by the fact that in recent years the population of Canada geese has greatly increased. But the waste produced by so many birds has fouled rivers and caused algae levels to spike in ponds and lakes.
- US production of oil has led to lower energy prices, which has certainly benefited consumers and businesses. It has also lessened our reliance on foreign oil. But the increase in production is largely due to fracking, a geological process that many scientists believe will have damaging ecological consequences.
- It's a commonly accepted notion that the colonists rose up in unison against the tyranny of the British, but the truth is more complicated than that. In fact, only one-third of the colonists wanted independence. One-third of the colonists remained loyal to the British, while the other third was undecided.

- Several historians have argued that dropping the atomic bomb brought an end to World War II and may have saved a million lives. However, it's also true that the bombs that fell on Hiroshima and Nagasaki killed at least tens of thousands of innocent civilians, including many children and elderly people.

Strong nonfiction, then, doesn't strive to tie everything up in a neat bow, or reduce it to a sound bite. Rather, it must respect its subject by reflecting its complexity.

Wonderment and Awe

My remembrances of profound awe draw on powerful visual memories. I flash on my brother Jim, emerging from a shack in the woods and gleefully brandishing two handfuls of snakes, waving them in the air like some kind of modern-day Medusa. It was a heart-stopping moment. I felt sheer electric awe jolt through me before words had a chance to rush in, name, and logically explain what was going on.

Young children are replete with wonder but for some reason our stockpiles get gradually consumed as we're assimilated into mainstream society. I remember the time I took my sister Carolyn to JFK airport when she was five years old.

"Just look at this beautiful building!" she softly exclaimed as we walked through the terminal. "It's completely made out of glass!"

"You're right," I muttered. I'd visited that airport so many times, I'd stopped noticing the glass.

To embrace awe and wonder we need to rediscover that part of ourselves that still marvels at the world. But the place for awe and wonder in today's classroom is shaky at best. Too many school systems prize competency—knowing the right answer—above everything else. I worked in a fifth-grade class where the kids had been studying the passenger pigeon.

"There were more passenger pigeons than any other bird in America," Brian said. "There were billions of birds but they still got wiped out. That's amazing!"

"That's not amazing," Trevor replied, frowning. "Dude, we learned all that a month ago."

"It's a fact, true, but it's still pretty amazing," the teacher interjected. "I think Brian's right. How could a species with that many birds go extinct so fast? It still blows me away."

It's an excellent point. Being knowledgeable shouldn't erase wonderment. In fact, the opposite is usually true. My friend Bruce Derr plays lap steel guitar. Bruce knows more about guitars than I will ever know, yet he still marvels at the beautiful detail work found on certain instruments. "They just don't do that kind of work anymore," he told me.

David Perkins, who worked at Project Zero at Harvard, makes an intriguing distinction between *wondering about* and *wondering at*.

"To *wonder about* something is to have curiosity and pose questions about it," Perkins told me. "To *wonder at* something is to marvel at it."

Perkins develops this idea in his book *Future Wise*: "Wondering at provides us with an inspiration for wondering about the unknown. . . . Big questions can be insightfully analytical but not very inspirational unless backed by a sense of wonder" (2014, 77).

As an example Perkins asks us to consider this question: what are the three causes of the Industrial Revolution?

"The Industrial Revolution was an amazing game-changer, but the form of the question undermines wondering at," Perkins writes. "Asking for the three causes suggests that what's wanted is not so much free-flowing inquiry but a bottled answer" (2014, 77).

The best nonfiction contains both wondering about and wondering at. I found an excellent example on the front page of the *Boston Globe* in an article about the migration of the blackpoll warbler. Each of these tiny birds undertakes an incredible journey of up to 1,700 miles.

The slight birds, which typically weigh a little more than two quarters, accomplish this seemingly impossible feat by fattening up preflight, in some cases nearly doubling their body weight.

"They really just turn into flying machines," said William DeLuca, a research fellow at UMass who led the study published Wednesday in the journal Biology Letters. *"Fuel and wings and a little navigation chip in their head." (*Johnson 2015)

It's not that *wondering at* should trump *wondering about*; rather, they should enhance each other. Strong nonfiction demystifies a particular subject even as it remystifies it, never letting us forget the beauty and terror of the world in which we live.

Part 2

MAKING NONFICTION IN
THE CLASSROOM

Chapter 5

CHOOSING CHOICE

Remember the songbirds? I do. When I was a kid I could hear songbirds by the thousand when they swept through the Northeast on their yearly migration. All those different species, each with its own particular call, braided together to create rich, thronging music. For a few weeks each spring the skies around my house became a river of song.

Alas, that river has largely dried up. As any birder can tell you, the songbird population suffered a precipitous decline in the 1970s and 1980s. Tropical rain forests were cut down, shrinking habitats and giving birds fewer places to winter. Today the songbird population in North America has diminished significantly, representing but a small percentage of what it once was. The skies have largely fallen silent.

A similar phenomenon has happened in the writing classroom. Today when I venture into a classroom to watch a room full of young writers at work, I often sense a lack of energy, juice, oomph. It seems like many students are just going through the motions.

Teaching writing has never been easy, but it wasn't too long ago when kids really enjoyed writing. You could *feel* their enthusiasm. Many times in a New York City public school I'd walk into a classroom and find myself greeted by spontaneous applause. The kids were delighted to see me because my appearance signaled a special occasion—writing! They couldn't wait to start putting pencil to paper. In those classrooms young writers got the time and the opportunity to play with language. Teachers delighted in the inventiveness of their young writers, many of whom created their own forms. One first grader devised a poetic form he called the "Oh"—"Oh to the Sun," and "Oh to the Wind"—that made everybody laugh.

What happened to the joy of writing?

"We've done a great job of sucking the joy out of the writing classroom," one fifth-grade teacher remarked to me recently.

Why? How? What pedagogical rain forests got cut down to create such a diminished habitat for writing? While there are many possible suspects, I'd finger choice—or, to be precise, the lack of it—in the writing classroom.

The writing workshop needs to belong to the students—not just to us. It has to feel like their thing—not just ours. There's so little in school that students truly own. The writing workshop used to be a place students owned, but is that still true? Choice is not quite extinct, but it has been pared back so much that what we think of as choice is but a dim shadow of what it once was and what it could still be. Nowadays I'm dismayed to find many writing workshops dominated by elements such as these:

Test preparation. I've been to many districts where students do test practice in writing as often as once a week.

Curricular mandates. Too many schools direct students to assigned writing as part of some curricular mandate, such as character education.

Common Core State Standards. I worked with a group of teachers and administrators at a large urban school. The principal had decorated a spacious room to make it attractive and conducive to professional development. Around the room was a series of bulletin boards displaying student writing, each one with one of the Common Core standards, neatly typed, at the center. While I understand the impetus for this arrangement, this visual arrangement gave me pause and helped clarify my own thinking. Shouldn't we put the students' writing—not the standards—at the epicenter of our work?

Genre studies and units of study. Like modular furniture, such units have become widely used, so much so that it's becoming difficult to find schools that don't use them. To be fair, I will acknowledge that such writing units have value. Many are content-rich and draw on real-world models, giving students important information they need to write well in a genre. And they provide important scaffolding to new writing teachers. But there's no question that these proliferating units have eroded the element of choice—both for young writers and for teachers. In the unit-of-study world, genre gets taught in a top-down way. It's hard to imagine students having the opportunity to generate an idea and follow it to the most appropriate genre.

Imagine a fourth-grade teacher leading his class through a unit on feature articles. In that class there's a slender boy, Ramon, whose uncle has just died. That event is foremost in Ramon's world and he wants to write about it. However, the class is working through a unit on persuasive writing, so Ramon must wait.

Recently the language arts coordinator in a high-achieving school asked me to review their writing curriculum for fourth and fifth grades. There was a month devoted to feature articles, a month devoted to persuasive essays, a month of expository writing, several weeks devoted to test preparation, and on and on throughout the year. I tried to look at this calendar through the eyes of a ten-year-old student, particularly a boy. True, there was a chunk of time allocated for memoir, and two weeks were designated for writing poetry. But all in all, that writing calendar didn't look like a whole lot of fun.

Young writers thrive in a classroom where they have choice, and I mean this in the fullest sense of the word: choice of genre, choice of topic, choice in how they decide to create a piece of writing. We have created this elaborate contraption called the writing/reading workshop. Choice is the crank that turns the machine and brings it alive. So much is "done to" students in school. Workshop is that one rare place where students get to do the doing. Students need choice in all kinds of writing, and especially with a genre like nonfiction.

Choice in Nonfiction Writing

When students delve into information writing they must venture away from their selves, their personal stories, in order to discover and explain the world at large. Some kids find this transition from self to world difficult. One way to make it smoother is to encourage them to choose nonfiction topics they know something about.

Imagine you and your friends visit a large flea market. It's a big ramshackle affair with aisles upon aisles and mountains of stuff. Where on earth do you start? One of your friends makes a beeline for the vinyl records (a hobby of his). Another friend goes to the antique glassware (she collects it). Still another starts poring through stalls with vintage dolls and doll clothing.

This kind of shopping is anything but random. People are drawn to what interests them. This abiding interest brings with it a level of familiarity and prior knowledge that, in turn, makes it possible for you to be a savvy shopper. You know from experience what you're looking for, what features are important, and what an item should cost.

Many professional writers will tell you that their interest in a particular subject is rooted in their personal history.

"My father owned a small plane when I was growing up, and I often flew with him," says author Louise Borden. "That's why I've written three books about aviation" (*Fly High! The Story of Bessie Coleman*; *Good-bye, Charles Lindbergh*; and *Touching the Sky: The Flying Adventures of Wilbur and Orville Wright*).

When you encourage students to choose their own topics, you might suggest that they start by making an expertise list. Ask them, "What subject are you an expert in?" Here's a sampling from the students in a fourth-grade class in North Andover, Massachusetts.

Brian: hockey

Melinda: horses

Tiffany: taking care of toddlers

Max: deer hunting

Patrick: fly-fishing

Nick: rock music, especially Led Zeppelin

I talked to one boy named Josh, who was slumped at his desk, an empty sheet of paper in front of him.

"What are you an expert in?" I asked.

He drummed the table. "Nothing."

I smiled. "I doubt that. C'mon, tell me something you know a lot about."

Suspiciously, Josh peered up at me. "Do you really want to know?"

"I really do."

"Professional wrestling," he blurted.

"You mean, like, WWF?"

"WWE," he corrected me. "That stands for World Wrestling Entertainment. I know all the rules, all the wrestlers, the different belts, titles, everything. My favorite wrestler is CM Punk. That guy is *awesome.*"

For the first time I detected energy, even excitement, in Josh's voice.

"Write that down," I urged. "You can write about that."

He blinked in surprise. "Really?"

"Really," I told him. "Teach me all about CM Punk."

Josh started to write. The teacher and I encouraged other kids to write about subjects that were near and dear to their hearts. When he and the other students in that class started working on their nonfiction pieces, they began with a level of familiarity based on a reservoir of prior knowledge. Certainly more research would still be required, but these kids already knew enough that they could "walk the walk and talk the talk" without feeling like imposters. The conditions were ripe for a successful writing experience.

You can energize a class of nonfiction writers by putting them in the driver's seat and inviting them to choose what they want to write about. It's especially important to let students choose their nonfiction topics early in the year when you first introduce them to this genre. But we shouldn't stop there. When it comes to choice in nonfiction writing, deciding what to write about is just the beginning. We need to empower students to make the important decisions that all nonfiction writers have to make, including these:

- How do I want to start? Do I want to use a traditional beginning, or might I fashion a more unusual lead?
- Might I structure this piece as a song, poem, or rap? (See Figure 5.1.)
- What is my purpose? To explain? Debunk commonly held myths about a subject? Give practical advice?
- Who is my audience?
- What tone do I want to take? Let's say I'm writing about colony collapse disorder, a plague that has decimated the population of honeybees in many parts of the country. Do I want to write with a funny, tongue-in-cheek kind of tone? Or do I want to produce

Bird Rap

by Taylor Curtis

If you think that
birds are jerks,
wait til you see
how their respiration works!

You see, I'm a bird,
I've got a feather coat,
I've got a glottis
in the back of my throat!

I don't have any sweat glands,
you say: "What a disaster!"
but when it comes to coolness
the bird is the master!

I've got these air sacs
that can't be beat,
with them I will not
overheat!

You see, I'm not weird,
I don't have two tongues,
I've got a trachea
that leads to my lungs.

I need a lot of energy,
(it isn't fair),
I use a lot of oxygen,
(just call it air!)

The air goes down the air sacs,
and I get oxygen,
and then it goes back through the lungs,
and it happens once again!

Of course I've got a larynx,
I do not have much choice,
but I've also got a syrinx,
which takes care of my voice!

Figure 5.1 "Bird Rap" poem

> *You're thinking: "Hurry up and finish!*
> *Come on while I'm still young!"*
> *and I guess it's really time to stop . . .*
> *Since now my song is done!*

Figure 5.1 "Bird Rap" poem (continued)

a piece of writing that's an urgent call to arms, something to get readers fired up?
- What sources will I use, and how many?
- What stories or revealing anecdotes might I include?
- Do I want to include interviews? With whom?
- What visuals—maps, charts, drawings, diagrams, photographs—would strengthen my piece and make this subject come alive for the reader?

Skilled chefs may glance at a recipe, or several of them, but they also give themselves permission to improvise. We could look at student nonfiction writing in a similar way. Certainly they will need guidance in making these decisions. What are some advantages in doing it a particular way? What is the downside? And, realistically, certain choices may not yield stellar results. But at least they can say with certainty that the writing they produce is their own.

Group Nonfiction Projects

This chapter is a ringing endorsement of the idea that students need to choose their own nonfiction topics. This begs the question: is there any place for a class working together on a nonfiction study or group project?

Certainly. One day a fourth-grade boy in Maine found an injured owl on the playground. His class immediately fell in love with this owl, adopted it, and nursed it back to health. This led to an impromptu investigation of owls, a project that involved all the students and lasted three weeks. The students and teacher learned that the injured creature was a barred owl, a species commonly found in the Northeast. This project gave the teacher an opportunity to guide students in how to conduct nonfiction research (including interviewing a local bird expert).

I'm all about classrooms that embrace kids' passions, but it's worth noting that a teacher's passion could also be the catalyst for a project or nonfiction investigation. In his book *An Ethic of Excellence*, Ron Berger describes a project in western Massachusetts that began as a collaboration with John Reid, a geology professor at Hampshire College. Ron and John wanted to study the quality of water wells in a local town using a mass spectrometer. Ron told his fifth-grade class what this study would entail and asked if they wanted to participate. The kids said yes. Berger describes the project like this:

> *Once the well project began, the classroom was transformed. The days were filled with preparing maps, surveys, data forms, instruction sheets; labeling and packing sterile bottles and test kits; planning meetings, developing distribution protocols and testing schedules. There were lessons in science, math, writing, technology, and politics . . . Much of the time, students came in to school, checked in like workers in a business, and got down to work writing, editing, organizing, packing, and preparing endless graphs and tables. Many days I had to force them to leave the computers and get to lunch.* (2003, 112)

I wouldn't frame this issue as a matter of choice versus assigned writing. There's no doubt that those fifth graders got immersed in real-world nonfiction. Such a rich experience! A group project like this has undeniable value and works as a rehearsal for the individual work they will have to do later. A healthy classroom should have a balance of individual and whole-class work, both in reading and in writing. (See Figure 5.2.)

Whole-class reading	Individual reading
Whole-class writing	Individual writing

Figure 5.2 Individual and whole-class reading/writing chart

There's at least one additional benefit to a project like the one Ron Berger describes. Today's workplace puts a premium on being able to work collaboratively on a team or in a small group. A project like this helps facilitate the interpersonal skills students will need to collaborate in an effective manner.

Opening up choice is not a cure-all for all the woes in your writing workshop, but it will help reenergize it. Once students realize that they're the ones making the crucial decisions in their writing, don't be surprised if there's a new feeling in your class. Giving student writers real choice will go a long way toward bringing zest, passion, and joyfulness back into the writing classroom. With those conditions in place they can make dramatic strides to grow into stronger writers.

Chapter 6

WHERE HAVE ALL THE NONFICTION READ-ALOUDS GONE?

"**W**hen we read great literature to children we are filling the storehouse," author Bill Martin Jr. once remarked to me. This peculiar phrase—*filling the storehouse*—rumbles around in my head even to this day. I believe Bill Martin meant this: reading to children allows them to soak up unmeasurable richness—plot possibilities, detail, story structures, language play, mood, character types, vocabulary, an expectation of pleasure, a sense of tension/resolution—all the important tools they'll need to grow into stronger readers.

But reading to students also nourishes them as *writers*. Students cannot write in a vacuum. In order to write well in any genre they need to have an image of what this writing looks and feels and sounds like. The writing in a classroom can only be as strong as the literature that surrounds and supports and buoys it up. This idea applies to any genre—memoir, poetry, informal essay—but it's particularly true for nonfiction. Students may be well versed in fairy tales, fables, poetry, or realistic fiction, but their knowledge of nonfiction is often thin. It's our job to help them get familiar enough with this genre to have success when they write it.

We need to marinate students in the best nonfiction we can find. I'm choosing this verb deliberately, and not merely because it's consistent with the gastronomic imagery in this book. When we surround students with strong nonfiction, and give them enough time to think, read, reread, and talk, the power of that literature can soak into them. I've seen it countless times: strong literature really can transform young writers. It won't happen overnight, but introducing students to excellent models ultimately will lift the quality of the nonfiction those students create.

The Impact of the Whole-Class Read-Aloud

The read-aloud is the simplest, most direct way to bring nonfiction to your students. This idea isn't exactly new. Indeed the whole-class read-aloud has been praised, plumbed, and probed by many educators (Mary Hahn and Lester Laminack, among others). It's hard to be against reading aloud, because the benefits are indisputable. When we read aloud we show students how a skilled reader would approach this, or any, nonfiction text. The read-aloud gives students the opportunity to hear a difficult text read with fluency. During a read-aloud we can stop, think aloud, and make our thinking visible. We can model habits and strategies used by people who read nonfiction. A read-aloud creates an elegant yet almost invisible scaffolding, a rich opportunity for you to hold hands with your students, assisting them as they venture into more difficult subject matter. This will be particularly important when they dig in to a challenging genre like nonfiction.

"Nonfiction often has rich, domain-specific vocabulary," Robert Pondiscio, senior fellow and Vice President for External Affairs at the Thomas B. Fordham Institute, points out. "You're more likely to hear words like 'orbit,' 'zenith,' 'solar,' or 'celestial' in a book on astronomy. Read-alouds not only grow vocabulary, they are the best way to build critical background knowledge, which is essential for later reading comprehension" (2012).

Choosing a story or fable for a read-aloud? Check. Selecting a poem? Check. But something odd happens when it comes to reading aloud nonfiction. For the most part, we don't. It's akin to stretching before working out—we all know we should stretch, but we don't get around to doing it. After talking to many teachers, literacy coaches, principals, and educators, I've come to the surprising conclusion that they don't typically choose nonfiction for their read-alouds.

So why don't they? Maybe they themselves don't feel comfortable with nonfiction. Or maybe it just doesn't seem as compelling as a storybook.

"As committed to nonfiction as I am now, I find it hard to fit in both (fiction and nonfiction)," says Franki Sibberson, coauthor of *Still*

Learning to Read: Teaching Students in Grades K–6 (2003). "I find that I have to make a strong effort to find quality accessible nonfiction and to read it aloud."

I shared my perceptions about the scarcity of nonfiction read-alouds with Lester Laminack, the author of *Unwrapping the Read Aloud: Making Every Read Aloud Intentional and Instructional.*

"We have seen the power of reading aloud an engaging story, a provocative poem, or a fluid narrative," Lester said. "Less often do we find teachers routinely sharing well-crafted nonfiction, which is too bad. If we expect young readers and writers to be drawn into nonfiction, we must bring them to the pages with the same love of language, the same passion for print that we demonstrate for fiction. I encourage teachers to harness the power of read aloud to build familiarity, comfort, interest, and competence in students as readers and writers of nonfiction."

A few commonsense guidelines for reading nonfiction aloud:

- Share your connection to/interest in the subject before you begin reading aloud the book.
- Don't belabor text features. With nonfiction there's a temptation to point out text features, and while there are benefits to that, doing so can interrupt the rhythm of the book. Let's not rob students from the pleasure of the book.
- Don't teach too much vocabulary ahead of time. The Common Core State Standards warn against "front-loading" vocabulary; I agree. As much as possible, teach vocabulary in the context of the book itself.
- Make the read-aloud a pleasurable experience.
- Emphasize the narrative aspects of the book (characters, problems, trouble, and triumph) as much as the factual information.
- Give time for kids to talk about/react to what you have read. It's tempting to rush in with our pearls of wisdom, but wait time is important here. Students need time to put their own language to what they have heard. If students are given the chance to react to the book they will tend to respond to it holistically, which is the appropriate place to start.

There are many places to find titles for a nonfiction read-aloud. The Orbis Pictus Award, given every year for outstanding books of nonfiction, is a great place to start (http://www.ncte.org/awards/ Orbispictus). Your librarian will also have suggestions. Here's a short list to get you started.

Some Nonfiction Read-Aloud Suggestions

Where the Forest Meets the Sea by Jeannie Baker

On a Beam of Light: The Story of Albert Einstein by Jennifer Berne

A River of Words: The Story of William Carlos Williams by Jen Bryant

The Great Kapok Tree: A Tale of the Amazon Rain Forest by Lynne Cherry

Extreme Animals: The Toughest Creatures on Earth by Nicola Davies

14 Cows for America by Carmen Agra Deedy

Tornadoes! by Gail Gibbons

The Man Who Walked Between Two Towers . . . And More Inspiring Tales by Mordecai Gerstein

Can We Save the Tiger? by Martin Jenkins

Born to Be Giants: How Baby Dinosaurs Grew to Rule the World by Lita Judge

Fireboat: The Heroic Adventures of the John K. Harvey by Maira Kalman

Wilma Unlimited: How Wilma Rudolph Became the World's Fastest Woman by Kathleen Krull

The Scoop on Poop! The Fascinating Science of How Animals Use Poop by Wayne Lynch

The Great Fire by Jim Murphy

Animals Nobody Loves by Seymour Simon

Reading Individually or with a Partner

I have emphasized the read-aloud as a way to bring nonfiction to students and help them develop a deeper understanding of this genre, but of course the whole-class read-aloud is only one way of doing so. Teachers should also structure time for kids to read nonfiction books individually or with a partner. Encourage students to get into pairs to study a nonfiction book. If the text is a picture book, they might decide to read the book aloud. We may devalue the conspiratorial cross-talk that takes place while two boys look at a dinosaur book, but I've observed that when kids pore over a nonfiction book, nine times out of ten they are deeply engaged, on-task. The comments they make after reading the book indicate that they gave it a close reading indeed. (Often they pay as much attention to the illustrations as they do to the text.) After they have read the book, you might have them fill out some facsimile of the criteria list in Figure 6.1 and make time for them to report their findings to the class.

Figure 6.1 Classroom Connection
Making a Criteria List

A criteria list is a great way to study, identify, and clarify the craft moves or techniques used by nonfiction writers. It will help you move the conversation from the "what" of the nonfiction book (which is specific) to the "how" (craft) of the book (which is generalizable).

Use a large anchor chart and a marker. If possible, set it up horizontally (landscape) and mark off three columns. As students read nonfiction books, individually or during a read-aloud, you can start filling in this chart.

Book Title	Craft/Strategy	Why Did Author Use It?
Diary of a Worm by Doreen Cronin	Diary	Lets us imagine a worm's thoughts and feelings. Makes us feel connected to it.

A criteria list like this will add to your students' repertoire of craft and help them realize that a strategy used by one author isn't limited to that one book, but could be used in any piece of nonfiction. Furthermore, it provides the perfect opportunity to remind students of strategies they can use to write their own nonfiction.

Which one is preferable: the whole-class read-aloud or having kids read books individually or in small groups? This shouldn't be an either/or proposition; indeed there's no reason why both couldn't take place within your classroom. They both have value, because they allow students to become savvier about nonfiction in different ways.

Eventually we want to steer the conversation from the "what" of the nonfiction book (which is specific) to the "how" (craft) of the book (which is generalizable to the genre as a whole). Time pressure might tempt us to hurry this transition, but it's important to let this transition happen naturally, and not force it. One of the intrinsic appeals of nonfiction is the allure and the Ripley's Believe It or Not awesomeness of the real world. Kids need ample time to savor this so they can fall under the mesmerizing spell of the real.

Chapter 7

AN EXPLORATORY NOTEBOOK

Students should be learning a strong and unpretentious prose that will carry their thoughts about the world they live in.
—William Zinsser, *Writing to Learn*

About twenty years ago I coached soccer. Back then I was given a roster, a schedule, six orange cones, and two soccer balls. I discovered that two balls didn't go very far when I was trying to run drills for a dozen kids. The kids on my team spent way too much time waiting in line until it was their turn.

The current thinking in this regard has changed. Today it is believed that young athletes need to touch/handle the ball as much as possible in order to improve their skills. (In basketball, the best athletes handle the ball up to 75 percent of the time. No wonder they seem so comfortable and skillful!) Nowadays a soccer coach might receive a large net bag that contains eight or ten balls. You break your kids into pairs and give each pair a ball. That way, each player spends most of the time handling the ball—kicking, dribbling, trapping—instead of waiting around.

I intend to connect this sports story to nonfiction writing, and I'll do so by tapping into an idea first proposed by the great William Zinsser in his book *Writing to Learn* (1993). In that book Zinsser talks about two kinds of writing: Type A and Type B. Type A writing is finished, authoritative nonfiction. When we read a magazine or nonfiction book we are reading Type A writing, where the author displays expertise. By contrast, Type B writing is tentative, exploratory. Type B writing can help us think our way into an understanding of the topic.

Picture a large iceberg floating in the ocean (Figure 7.1). It is an impressive sight: the massive size, the crisp whiteness against the blue sea. And yet what we see represents about 10 to 15 percent of the whole iceberg. The much larger underbulk stays hidden below the surface. In the same way, a reader may never actually see any Type B writing, but it will inform the final piece. Generating it is an important, even necessary part of the process if the writer hopes to produce writing that is substantial as well as readable.

Figure 7.1 Iceberg

Zinsser goes a step further and suggests that one reason our students' nonfiction writing sounds so forced and stilted is that we rush them to produce Type A writing before they have done enough Type B writing. They aren't sufficiently comfortable or fluent with their topics to be able to communicate as true insiders.

In this chapter I'll propose a few kinds of Type B writing you might try with your students. As you look at the list that follows, remember that these are meant to be suggestions only. Not every one of these ideas will resonate with your students. Also, feel free to add to this list. Students will need to have a container for this kind of tentative thinking—let's call it an Exploratory Notebook. I'd suggest something slender, no more than twenty or thirty blank pages, to hold this kind of tentative thinking.

Write Down What You Already Know

When we learn about our world we don't pour this new knowledge into an empty vessel. Whatever we learn mixes with what we already knew about this subject. If you allow students to choose their topic, there's a high likelihood that they will choose a nonfiction subject about which they already have some knowledge.

Encourage your students to begin by jotting down what they already know. When students activate their prior knowledge they quickly realize they're not starting from square one; it may surprise them to discover that they know more than they realized about the topic.

Don't expect students to use complete sentences or coherent paragraphs in the Exploratory Notebook. The purpose here is to use writing to generate thinking. A bulleted list will suffice.

Generate Questions, Wonderings, and Speculations

My book *Boy Writers: Reclaiming Their Voices* (2006) began with a question: why are boys struggling in writing classrooms? This question begat a host of others. Are girls naturally better writers than boys? Does writing workshop somehow marginalize boys? How? Could the fact that elementary school teachers are predominantly female have something to do with it?

Encourage students to use the Exploratory Notebook to list questions they have about their subjects. After doing so they might put a star next to what seem to be the most important questions.

"When kids write nonfiction we often embrace an 'answer culture,'" Barry Lane, author of *After "The End,"* told me. "In a question culture, we value questions as tools of true inquiry. At the same time, we signal to students that some facts are more important than others."

Chunk Out Your Topic

I'm not a huge fan of giving kids detailed outlines for their nonfiction projects. Still, the question remains: how can students organize their material so that it's clear and sensible to the reader?

As students begin gathering information about their subject they'll begin to see that it falls into various categories. A student writing about the Brazilian rain forest might find these sections:

1. Benefits of the rain forest (producing oxygen, cooling the earth, medicines derived from native plants that grow there)

2. Destruction of the rain forest: rates of deforestation and why this is taking place

3. What we can do to protect what rain forest remains

The student could devote a particular page to facts about benefits, another page to facts about destruction, and so forth. Breaking a topic into chunks in this way will help the student with organization as he or she begins to think about how to move from Type B writing to Type A (public) writing.

Make a Web or Visual Representation of a Topic

Upper-grade writing classrooms tend to be "wordcentric," which benefits a certain kind of learner but inhibits another. Some people really do process information better when they can use visuals instead of words. The Exploratory Notebook is a great place for kids to sketch, draw, and doodle. Encourage them to draw maps, artifacts (e.g., weapons), clothing, and other relevant details.

Collect Surprising Facts, Stats, and Information

Some tarantulas throw their hair at an enemy. Molten lava has a temperature of around 2,000 degrees Fahrenheit. An elephant's trunk contains more than 40,000 muscles. I figure that I'm similar to other people, so if a fact intrigues or amazes me there's a good chance my readers will have a similar reaction.

React to What You Are Learning

"Dump-truck writing" has long been the MO for students who struggle to produce informational writing. They grab facts from a website and dump them—*CLUNK!*—into their report. No wonder the writing comes out sounding stilted and voiceless. But there's another problem. Sometimes when students learn about the nonfiction world they become passive or even jaded.

"My students had been studying about the Holocaust," one seventh-grade teacher told me. "First we read Anne Frank's diary. Then we read *Night* by Elie Wiesel. After a while they seemed almost numbed by the Holocaust. We'd read accounts of the massacres of Jews in the Polish ghettos, and my students barely reacted."

One way to push students off this passive stance is to encourage them to react to what they are learning. I worked with one teacher who has her students list facts on the left-hand side of the notebook. Then she directs them to react to those facts on the right-hand side, jotting down what amazes or appalls them about what they have learned.

Make a Prediction

Invite your students to predict what they're going to learn—even before they have learned it. Doing so is one more way to help your students take an active stance as they learn about their topic.

My friend Miranda teaches sixth-grade English in Illinois. She and her students had been studying the Civil War, and she announced that they would be watching a short video in class about the causes of that war. The students smiled when they heard this news. No work that day—movie time! She saw their body language, kicking back in anticipation of watching a film. Surely some of them would close their eyes in the darkened classroom.

"But before we watch the video I want you to write a brief paragraph," she told her students. "What do you think were the main causes of the Civil War?"

"But . . . I . . . I thought we were going to watch a video," one boy sputtered.

"Write your paragraph first," she told him. "I'll give you five minutes."

After the students wrote, Miranda dimmed the lights and showed the video.

"They watched that film differently," Miranda told me. "Because they had already committed themselves on paper, they had a stake in what they would see. They weren't passive—anything but."

Collect New Words and Terms Specific to Your Subject

As soon as you start researching whales you encounter a lexicon of new, alien words: *ambergris, baleen, breach, echolocation, pod, phyto-plankton* . . . By *alien* I mean words not normally used in everyday life. Students must begin to get comfortable with this vocabulary. Alas, often they never get around to doing so. They may include some new words in their finished (Type A) nonfiction writing, but those feel like gobs of flour that have not been fully mixed into the pancake batter. In other words, the new vocabulary is not fully integrated into the text.

In the Exploratory Notebook we can invite students to start collecting new words, phrases, and expressions that are particular to their subjects. Encourage them to explain these terms using their own words. You might brainstorm ways for students to explain these words (using a glossary, drawings, bubbles, or boxes) to their readers.

Sift and Sort

Young researchers will dig up lots of information, some of it highly pertinent, some irrelevant. They need to do two things: (1) understand the relative importance of various facts and (2) be able to explain it to an outside reader. The Exploratory Notebook can help in this regard.

Kaitlyn, a fourth grader, was writing a biographical piece about Thomas Jefferson. In her Exploratory Notebook I found a page she had titled "Important Facts." At the top of one page she had written, "Older Brother Dies on August 7, 1815." On the bottom of another page, buried in her notebook, she had jotted, "Wrote the Declaration of Independence in 1776." I asked her about it.

"Which do you think is more important?" I asked Kaitlyn.

Kaitlyn's lower lip trembled. "When his brother died. I love my brother, and if he died I . . . I . . . I don't know what I'd do."

Although we might acknowledge the emotional truth of Kaitlyn's conclusion, I think we'd all agree that in historic terms one event carries much more importance than the other, and we'd want Kaitlyn to understand that.

Students should be doing lots of rereading as well as writing in their Exploratory Notebooks. As they reread the lists of facts they've collected, you might suggest that they put a star or asterisk next to the most important ones. A highlighter would work, too. Or they could use a simple numerical system to start sorting facts:

1. most important
2. fairly important
3. less important

Try a "Flashdraft" on the Topic

This strategy draws on a student's comfort and familiarity with story. Invite your students to take what they're writing about and put it in brief narrative form—that is, embed it in a story.

> *When darkness falls, and the moon is not too bright, a mother sea turtle crawls out of the water and onto the beach. It's the same beach where she was born. She uses her hind legs to dig a hole in the sand about six inches deep. Then she squats down and begins laying her eggs. It takes her about two hours because she lays over a hundred of them, each one about the size of a ping pong ball. When she's finished she covers the eggs with sand. Finally she walks back to the water and swims away.*

Keeping an Exploratory Notebook will help students gain a deeper understanding of their subjects and give them the chance to write in an informal way. We need to give students lots of opportunities to use low-stakes writing in this regard. The suggestions provided here (and others you come up with) will give students various "touches" with their topics. Ultimately this will improve the quality of their expertise writing. When students are writing nonfiction this notebook can become part of the writing classroom. Share time should not be reserved only for finished pieces—students could also share from their Exploratory Notebooks.

But let's be careful about how we incorporate the Exploratory Notebook into the classroom. Kids have a finely tuned detector for busywork or writing-because-my-teacher-said-we-have-to-do-this. If the Exploratory Notebook is going to be meaningful for your students it has to have intellectual integrity. It's vital that they see it as authentic, flexible, and optional. One telling sign that your students find true value in the Exploratory Notebook is when they start coming up with their own ways of using it. When that happens, you know they have really occupied this idea and made it their own.

Chapter 8

BUILDiNG DEEP KNOWLEDGE

A powerful, rich draft grows from abundant soil.
　　　　　　　　　—Don Murray, *The Craft of Revision*

A few years ago I created a nonfiction piece for students, "Interview with a Coho Salmon," for my book *Mentor Author, Mentor Texts* (2011). I wanted to use a mock interview as a vehicle to explain the life cycle of a salmon. I started by imagining a character, a female salmon, a particular fish with her own personality. Since my audience would be young readers, I tried to incorporate humor wherever possible. Writing the final draft was actually enjoyable; I marveled at how easily it all came together. I'm sure it's because I had spent time researching the Coho salmon—its habitat, habits, love life, food, predators, etc. I knew that fish inside and out, so I had a wealth of information at my fingertips to draw on for the finished article.

This reflects the process I used as a freelance writer. The articles I wrote focused on a wide variety of topics but writing them always followed the same routine. I spent the first chunk of time taking a crash course in whatever I was writing about. I dug up facts, learned, soaked in the new world, and became a magnet for anything I could find on the subject.

Networking? You bet. I talked to friends and explained to them what I was writing about. They, in turn, connected me to people they knew who might be able to help me. I interviewed anybody who would talk to me, transcribed those interviews, and pored over the transcripts, searching for revealing or insightful quotes. I collected facts, stats, and oddities.

Throwing myself into the particulars of a subject often felt abrupt and disorienting. Still, it helped me develop a familiarity, a comfort level, with what I'd be writing about. During the process I could feel myself moving gradually from outsider to insider status until, finally, I was ready to take a stab at writing a first draft. (Incidentally, I hoped to make the same outsider-to-insider transformation in my readers.) This feeling of fullness, readiness, confidence—*I know I'm ready to write about this*—is crucial, but I couldn't have gotten there without all the learning I'd just done.

Any nonfiction writer needs to have a range of skills, including how to research, read critically, and take notes. (See Figure 8.1.) How do we help students develop the skills they'll need to create strong nonfiction?

Figure 8.1 Classroom Connection
Taking Notes During Research

For the past few years Dr. Cyrene Wells has worked as a volunteer in Lisa Bartlett's eighth-grade language arts class at the Elm Street School in East Machias, Maine. Cyrene and Lisa spend time teaching students how to take notes when researching a topic. Here Cyrene shares her thoughts on the topic.

We start with the basic question: Why do we take notes? Usually someone says something like, "It helps me remember." (Honest kids admit, "Because the teacher collects them.") I tell kids that taking notes is a way of reminding me about what I know about a topic. I don't want to start writing with only the most recent research in my head.

We have a projector and screen so that kids can see my work up close. I devote a couple of mini-lessons during the most intense time of researching; I also share note taking/note using as the writing continues. A lot of what follows happens not in lessons, but through quick, "by-the-way" reminders.

I show them my sticky notes in the books I've read. Then I show my notes taken from those sticky-noted pages, though I explain that I don't like to slow down to take notes while I read. Some kids tell me it doesn't work that way for them, that they actually like to interrupt their reading with note taking. I think they are saying that they get bored by reading nonfiction in long stretches.

I tell them that I like to mark up text, showing them notes and stars and lines in the margin for important things. I show them how I number articles printed out from the Internet so that I can just circle numbers in my notes. I show them highlighted places, but warn them that a completely highlighted text is pretty useless. They need to start making decisions about what information is important and what is not. When we first begin researching a topic everything seems new and important. After researching more broadly we see that some things matter more than others. They can always go back later with a different color highlighter or pen.

We talk about the advantage of taking notes from YouTube or other videos, how you can stop the video to jot a note. I show them my notes from interviews. We show how to bullet items and to leave spaces between pieces of information so that notes are more easily readable.

I show them my notebook for taking notes on notes, using headers like "What do I know?" and "Things I don't want to leave out" and "More questions." I also show them how I take notes on only one side of the paper in my notebook so that I can make notes/questions/arrows on the opposite blank page as I go along. I show them how I sometimes highlight and sticky-note my notes. I like to show kids about notes on notes (though most of them do it themselves). We talk about taking notes using their own words so that someone else's words don't show up (plagiarism) in the final writing.

Lisa and I aren't the ones who do all the teaching. The kids show Lisa and me and the rest of the class about bookmarking websites. They demonstrate how some of them prefer to take notes on their computers. Always, we invite kids to share their strategies with their whole class. The projector and screen makes this easy. Sometimes I think the kids pay more attention to each other than they do to us!

We also have a lesson about not getting stuck in the research and having to move on from major note taking. I've done this in my own research so I recognize it in others. I love collecting information, making lists, looking for more sources. But if we're not careful, the research can become an end in itself. We can get stuck in it—it can be way easier than writing! It's important to remember that we are researching for a purpose.

I explain it to students like this: "You'll need money in the bank (your research) to get going, but you'll undoubtedly make more deposits as you go along."

We don't collect their notes, but each day they turn in a sheet, briefly explaining what they did that day, and during the research-intensive time of the study, we end class by going around, sharing cool things we learned during class.

Here's the most important thing—I research/write with the kids and share my processes with them. There aren't any templates. It seems to me that note taking depends on the bigger task. Our kids research for their multigenre projects, knowing that they will need information to drive various genres. A particular genre, and the topic itself, will demand certain kinds of information.

I talked about this with Penny Kittle. Penny is an English teacher, the author of *Book Love*, and an advocate dedicated to helping students and teachers develop a passion for reading and writing.

"Students can write well about their nonfiction topics only after they have built up a depth of knowledge about those topics," Penny declared.

This sounds wise, but in order for me to understand, I had to dig deeper. I wondered, how can we make this happen in the classroom? How can we help students build depth of knowledge so they can write about their subjects with fluency, ease, and a sense of confidence?

Immersion

When it comes to building knowledge, Penny has two goals for her students. She wants to help them get comfortable with what they are writing about, and at the same time she wants her students to increase their knowledge about the genre nonfiction. She often begins by leading her class through a study of feature articles. They explore the writing—style, quotations, organization, subheadings—found in print articles. In addition, they look closely at multimedia texts. For example, her students examined "Snow Fall: The Avalanche at Tunnel Creek," a multimedia piece published in the *New York Times* on December 20, 2012. They notice the various formats used for conveying information:

- Video or "minimovies" created with iMovie
- Google maps
- Charts
- Slide show of images

"Imitation is how all writers work," Penny tells her students. "If I want to write a poem, I read a bunch of poems to understand how they work. Sometimes I even follow the structure of them for a while, using my ideas on top of someone's structure. You will closely examine a multimedia article in order to imagine the one you will be writing."

Fiction That Feeds Nonfiction

Penny encourages her students to pick a topic they already know something about. As they begin wading in to their subject, she asks them to put together a reading list that includes the following:

Two nonfiction books about their topic

Two fiction books (usually historical fiction)

Her requirement that students include historical fiction surprised me, so I decided to ask her about it.

"One of my students was writing about the 9/11 attacks," Penny said. "She read George Bush's autobiography and she also read *Extremely Loud and Incredibly Close* by Jonathan Safran Foer. Another boy was writing about fear. He decided to read *Deadline* by Chris Crutcher, a book about a student who discovers he only has one year left to live."

Penny has found that reading historical fiction helps her students develop a sense of intimacy with their subjects. This notion surprised me at first, but the more I thought about it, the more it began to make sense. Reading fiction requires a leap of the imagination. Nonfiction writers know they must help their readers take a similar leap to understand the subject being written about. Reading fiction has an additional benefit—it gives the student more contact with a relevant topic; in other words, it affords them more "touches with the ball." It's a pleasurable way for students to delve deeper into what they're going to be writing about.

Practice

Penny posed a question to Elaine Miller, a researcher at the University of New Hampshire.

"What do you notice that incoming students can't do?"

Miller answered without hesitation. "They don't know how to write about and interpret raw material."

Elaine Miller was describing incoming college freshmen; however, I suspect teachers at all levels would agree with her assessment. Nowadays, with the abundance of readily available information, the ability to critically interpret data has become more important than ever. Indeed, the Common Core State Standards were constructed in an effort to improve students' ability in this area. Penny meets this challenge in several ways:

> **Notebook jottings.** She invites students to play (sketch, collect, hypothesize) with their topics in a writer's notebook. Smart nonfiction writers cast a wide net when they research; the writer's notebook gives students another way to collect.

> **Quick-writes.** "My students do quick-writes in every genre," Penny says. "We study charts, tables, and graphs and write from them while working on feature articles. I use controversial issues to have them practice arguing for/against ideas when we're studying argument. First I write and model revisions; then the students write and revise."

> Busywork: no. Practice writing: yes. The importance of practice is recognized in every field—acting, music, dance, athletics, the culinary arts—so why should writing be any different? Inviting students to do informal, low-stakes writing (no grades or harsh critiques) is a great way to help them build confidence as well as knowledge about their subjects.

Graph, charts, and table study. These formats, which often rely on numbers more than words, are common features of informational writing. But many students feel intimidated because they have little experience using and interpreting them.

"I get them to practice writing about raw information," Penny says. "For example, I ask them to create a claim based on two different charts and see if they can back it up. In biology I had kids writing about infographics in the subject they were studying (for example, cloning in the class working on the reproductive system) . . . I got them into pairs and put their writing up for the class to read, study, and critique. We do this in class day after day. I want them to get the feel for what nonfiction writing sounds like."

Penny mentions that she separates students into pairs. I'll admit that in the past I tended to discourage this kind of collaborative writing. I promoted writing as a solitary (and heroic) endeavor. But I've changed my thinking in this regard to why students *should* write together.

Passage Study

Passage study represents a kind of hands-on apprenticeship. It allows kids the opportunity to walk in the shoes of a highly skilled writer. Penny has found that passage study is a great way to stretch her writers and expose them to possibilities they might never have considered. This is another kind of directed practice, one that involves inviting students to imitate sentences created by skilled nonfiction writers. In Chapter 9, I describe a passage study I conducted with Linda Rief's eighth-grade students at the Oyster River Middle School in Durham, New Hampshire.

Oral Presentations

When Penny's students begin writing nonfiction she reminds them that they are "conducting, or directing a chorus." I was struck by these words, and invited Penny to unpack them.

Penny: I was talking about the way they need to direct a chorus of voices (their sources) and stay in charge of the central voice of the text. Young writers have a tendency to paste together quotes, but they don't maintain a central voice that uses those other voices to join their own. They need to add these other voices, but shouldn't give over their writing to them.

Ralph: Right. The reader gets a bunch of facts, but you don't have a sense that anybody's home.

Penny: Exactly. Sometimes I have to ask a student, "Where are *you* in this piece of writing?" I tell them, "It has to have the thread of your voice throughout."

Ralph: How do you help your students bring more of themselves into the nonfiction writing?

Penny: One thing that really helps is having them give an oral presentation. I have my students present their information to a panel of adults without using notes, sort of like a TED Talk.

Ralph: Does your class actually study TED Talks as a genre?

Penny: Yes! My students all created them in January and it was unbelievable. The best thing I've done in a while.

Ralph: Who is the audience? Do any adults come to listen?

Penny: I invited parents, teachers in our building, and teachers at our community college here in town.

Ralph: I imagine practicing to deliver their information orally, to a real audience, would go a long way toward helping them develop voice when it comes time for them to write.

Penny: Definitely. However, I should add that the voice they had in their talks didn't always end up in their writing.

Penny's approach rings true. She brings in exemplary models so students can build vision for what strong nonfiction looks and sounds like. She allots class time so students can talk and discuss these texts. Students get time to play and practice nonfiction writing. Penny is realistic; she doesn't expect her students to succeed in every one of their finished products. I was particularly intrigued to hear that she asks her students to read at least one piece of fiction related to their topic. This opens the door for students to experience pleasure as they research their subjects.

Chapter 9

PLUNGING INTO A NONFICTION TEXT STUDY

In Durham, New Hampshire, I visited several eighth-grade language arts classes at Oyster River Middle School. The teacher was Linda Rief, a friend and the author of several books, including *Read Write Teach* (2014). I brought along a nonfiction piece about the sport of skeleton, written by Rick Bragg and published in the *New York Times*. After Linda introduced me to the kids, I spoke to them.

"Rick Bragg is a celebrated writer and someone we can all learn from," I began. "Let's take a close look at this piece he wrote. I'll read it out loud. I encourage you to mark up the text while I'm reading it. Feel free to bracket your favorite parts. You might also underline or circle any part you find noteworthy in some way."

OLYMPICS: Skeleton Plunges Face-First Back into the Winter Games

SALT LAKE CITY, Feb. 17 — Picture riding the lid of a turkey roaster pan down a roller coaster rail after an ice storm.

Picture it at almost 80 miles an hour, with wicked turns, at G-forces so powerful that you cannot raise your helmet from the ice, which glitters just an inch away.

Now picture making that ride face first.

"I was screaming inside my helmet," said Chris Soule, as he described the first time he tried the ominous-sounding sport of skeleton. It returns to these Olympic Winter Games after a 54-year ban.

Soule, the 2002 World Cup gold medalist from Trumbull, Conn., says it is not as dangerous as it looks, sliding down a twisting, turning course belly down on a tiny sled, his helmeted head leading the way.

That may be, but whenever he tells the Olympic athletes in other sports what he is there for, they say much the same thing: "Oh. You guys are crazy."

Perhaps it is appropriate that international competitions for this event, perhaps the most perilous of all here, now begin with a moment of silence.

There is no affectation here, no baggy pants and thrash music like the snowboarders have, no ice skater's sequins and storied history, no cinematic skiing glory, acted out by a rugged Robert Redford, as in the downhill.

This is just fast and mean and a little bit insane, and if you mess up, if you are clumsy and brush the wall, there is pain and often blood. Soule used to wrap parts of his body in duct tape—the ice on the walls tended to eat his sweater off his arm.

Now, after petitioning Olympic officials to reinstate the sport— which gets its name because frames of earlier sleds resembled a skeleton—he and the rest of the world's most daring sliders will get a running start, hurl themselves and their sleds down a chute of hard ice and show the world what it means to ride the bones. The men's and women's competitions are scheduled for Wednesday.

"I haven't told my mother yet," said Lincoln DeWitt, one of Soule's Olympic teammates, when asked what his family thought of his competition here, which has been banned not once but twice from the Games.

It is a sport ruled, and abused, by gravity. (Bragg 2002)

"Okay, now I'd like you to get together and talk about the piece," I said. "What strikes you about this article? What is Rick Bragg doing well? What do you admire about the writing? Get with another person and talk about it."

Kids started talking in pairs and small groups about the article, tentatively at first, then louder and louder. After about five minutes I pulled the class back together for a whole-class discussion.

"I've had the luxury of reading this piece a bunch of times and I've got plenty to say about this article, but for now I'll try to keep quiet. I'm more interested in how you reacted to it and what you noticed."

One girl, Katie, shook her head. "The way he writes . . . you can tell it's a crazy sport."

"How?" I asked.

"By the way he describes it," she replied. "And the quotes he chooses."

Sarah agreed. "Yeah, at our table we got into a debate about which sport was more dangerous: skeleton, luge, or hockey."

This sparked an impromptu discussion, with many kids weighing in. I let it continue for a minute or so, and then regained control of the class.

"Okay, so what else did you notice?"

"Well, the writer didn't really express his own opinion," Nate put in. "I mean, he mostly tells what other people think."

This prompted a girl to raise her hand. "I disagree. He keeps bringing up how crazy it is. You can tell what he thinks by the details he chooses. And also by the language he uses—it's all dangerous."

"I guess, yeah," Nate admitted.

"This piece kind of surprised me," Abby put in. "Usually you'd expect an article like this to be mostly straight-up facts. But the way he writes it, it sounds more like a story."

Hannah zeroed in on this sentence: *Soule, the 2002 World Cup gold medalist from Trumbull, Conn., says it is not as dangerous as it looks, sliding down a twisting, turning course belly down on a tiny sled, his helmeted head leading the way.*

"The first part of the sentence talks about how the sport is not dangerous," she said. "But the second part convinces you that it *is* dangerous."

"Is the writer being, like, sarcastic?" Nate wondered aloud.

"Yes, or maybe ironic," I couldn't help adding.

He nodded. "Yeah."

At this point Linda Rief spoke up. "I was really struck by the lead. I think leads are so important. If you can come up with a lasting lead, it really sets the tone for the rest of the piece. This lead is so strong. Every word in that lead is doing important work."

"He uses a lot of short paragraphs," Anthony said.

"Yes," I agreed. "Why do you think he wrote it like that?"

Silence.

"Sometimes you know what you want to say," Riley muttered, "and you just say it."

I nodded. "That's true. Why else might he use a short paragraph?"

"They give you time to pause," Anthony put in. "Going to the next paragraph gives you time to think about what you just read."

"A sentence by itself can have a lot of impact," Abby added. "If it's surrounded by lots of other sentences you might miss it, but if you put it by itself it has more of an impact."

"Why?" I persisted.

"Well, it's easier to read," Owen said. "It makes you want to keep reading, and you can read faster."

Maddie raised her hand. "I noticed that at the beginning of the article he uses repetition. He keeps repeating the word *picture*."

"Why do you think he does that?"

She shrugged. "Well, it ties those sentences together. Even though they're in different paragraphs you can tell by that repeated word that they're connected."

"That makes sense," I replied. In fact, I'd never thought of that.

"Can we go back to the beginning?" another girl, Hannah, asked. "I mean, I was surprised when he writes about the turkey roasting lid. That detail is kind of . . . weird."

"Why do you think he chose it?"

"Maybe to exaggerate how small the sled is," Michael suggested. "It makes it feel more dangerous."

"It makes it seem like the rider is the turkey," Abby interjected.

Nate nodded. "Yeah, dead meat!"

Laughter.

I was impressed by how the kids were able to dig into Bragg's sentences and the structure of this piece. The thoughtful way they were able to speculate on the author's technique and intention was a testament to Linda's teaching. In some classes a discussion like this would quickly peter out; Linda's kids were able to sustain it for quite a while. It takes time for students to build stamina for a conversation like this, just as it does for writing.

I wanted to challenge the students to dig deeper into Rick Bragg's style by doing an exercise in which they would try to emulate one of the passages. Penny Kittle had mentioned to me that she does something similar with her high school students, so I decided to try it now. I asked the students to take a close look at these two sentences in Bragg's article.

There is no affectation here, no baggy pants and thrash music like the snowboarders have, no ice skater's sequins and storied history, no cinematic skiing glory, acted out by a rugged Robert Redford, as in the downhill. This is just fast and mean and a little bit insane, and if you mess up, if you are clumsy and brush the wall, there is pain and often blood.

I reread this passage out loud for the second time and asked, "What did you notice about this part?"

After a long pause David offered, "He's explaining about skeleton by telling us what it's *not*."

More discussion ensued. Kids mentioned other things:

- Tension between the first and last sentence
- List of things separated by commas
- Run-on sentences that go on and on

"Sometimes you can stretch yourself by trying to imitate what another writer is doing," I told the class. "Let's try that now. I'm going to challenge you to try to imitate what Bragg is doing in these sentences. But instead of writing about skeleton, write about your own topic. I'll tell you how I might do this. Let's say I wanted to create a historical piece about Martin Luther King, and I wanted to describe what it must have been like when he was in the Selma jail. In the spirit of Rick Bragg's sentences I might write this:

There is no luxury here, no soft featherbed you might find in a cozy inn or bed-and-breakfast, no tub where you could soak your tired bones after a long day of work. The jail cell is bare and cold and harsh and devoid of all human comfort, and if you forget all that, if you get too "uppity" and dare ask for a chair or extra blanket or anything to make your miserable existence a tiny bit more bearable, well, those unsmiling guards will be quick to remind you that the Selma jail is anything but a Holiday Inn.

The kids looked at me, thinking.

"Let's see what you come up with," I said. "Start by copying these two sentences down in your notebook. That's a good way to get a feel for what Rick Bragg is trying to do. Then see if you can write a few sentences of your own, based on your own topic, sentences that

Figure 9.1 Classroom Connection
Imitating a Writer's Style

This is an exercise designed to stretch your writers. Start by leading students through a brief study of an author and how he or she writes a nonfiction text. There are many great choices for this exercise. I find that *Are You a Bee?* by Judy Allen (2004) is a very accessible text for elementary-age students. (If you don't have this book, you can easily substitute any of the other books in the Backyard series.) In this book the narrator asks the reader to imagine life as a bee. The information about bees is transmitted through this lens. After you read this book aloud get students into pairs or small groups to discuss it. In whole-class discussion it's important for students to get a feel for not just the "what" of the book but also the "how."

Give your students time to imitate the technique used in this book, patterning their writing after Judy Allen's, substituting their own subjects for bees. When they have finished, make time for them to share. Remind students that they can use this technique in their own nonfiction writing.

emulate what Rick Bragg is doing in this passage." (See Figure 9.1.)

I gave the students seven minutes to write. Afterward I suggested they find someone and share what they'd written.

"Remember: we're just experimenting here," I reminded them. "These are just rough drafts, so let's be easy with each other."

The kids got into small groups to read what they'd written. Afterward I asked if anyone would be willing to share aloud with the whole class. Here's what Sara came up with:

There are no happy endings here. No concerned words. "I'm sorry. . . . Are you okay? . . . I'll make it up to you." No light voices. No warm embraces or sunrises. Only gray skies. There are dark blue eyes

Refusing another day. Our minutes contain heavy sighs, hollow laughter, drooping eyelids, and smiles that leave as quickly as they have come.

Abby wrote this:

Unlike other sports sailing doesn't require finesse. There is no smelly uniform, no team cheer before going into the water, not even a team that has your back. For the race, you are on your own, and if the other team gets ahead, so be it. There is a fire that fuels sailors, not unlike the one that burns in other sportsmen. Sailing requires a quick mind, strong arms, and like other sports, sailing is a way to drown your problems.

Implications and Take-Aways

The discussion was lively, especially in the second class I visited. This heartened me though I did notice that certain kids (girls) did most of the talking. Other kids seemed content to sit back and let their class-mates spin their theories. This suggests that I probably needed to structure more small-group talk time.

A potent mentor text is not a sheath (which holds one thing) but a quiver (which holds many). Even though I'd read this piece twenty times before, the kids still pointed out craft elements I'd never noticed—the repetition of the word *picture* in the first three lines, for instance. This surprised me. I thought I had found most of the craft elements in the piece.

In retrospect, I think that Linda's students probably could have benefited from more time with, and multiple readings of, the Rick Bragg article. Having to encounter a sophisticated new text and a strange man both at the same time (at 7:30 a.m.!) might have been a bit much. I wonder if we would have gotten more student involvement in the discussion if Linda had read the Rick Bragg the day before and sent it home with the students to read and think about. That way they would have been rereading the article with me, not encountering it for the first time. As a teacher, you walk the tightrope between belaboring a text (sucking all the juice out of it) and giving adequate time for kids to delve into and make it part of who they are.

Still, I was impressed by how willing and able students were to "put on the sweater" of Rick Bragg's passage and make it their own. They didn't do it exactly as I would have predicted—they borrowed more of the contrast than the rhythm of the long run-on sentences—but you can definitely see the influence of his writing on theirs. There's no doubt that Bragg's passage helped widen their repertoire for future writing projects, as would other strong models of nonfiction. They rode the energy of Rick Bragg's piece and let it take them to a place they couldn't have otherwise gone.

Chapter 10

THE POWER OF PRIMARY SOURCES

I'm looking for an arrowhead.
I want to hold one in my hand.
I want to touch the tip of history.
                        —Ralph Fletcher, from "Arrowhead"

Meet Ryan Prescott, a student from East Machias, Maine. He's in high school now but even as a small boy Ryan showed an intense curiosity about the world.

"I always read a lot," Ryan says. "When I was really little I got interested in the US presidents."

"He really wanted me to buy him this book about the presidents, but it was so expensive," his mother remembers. "He was three years old!"

Soon after that Ryan began to get interested in local history. His fourth-grade teacher, Mrs. Fulmer, had a similar passion.

"She taught me a lot about local Maine history, but not as part of the regular curriculum," Ryan says. "She taught it on the side. That was the only time I'd ever learned about local history. It's rare that I get a chance to talk about that—in school or out."

When Ryan was in eighth grade his English teachers were Lisa Bartlett and Dr. Cyrene Wells.

"Ryan was not particularly interested in grades," Cyrene remembers. "External motivation really wasn't a factor for him. He just wanted to do interesting things. Writing workshop, where he could choose his own topic, was a good fit for him."

Early that year Cyrene and Lisa decided to have their students experiment with multigenre writing, a concept developed by Tom Romano (2000, 2013). Instead of writing one long report on a topic, students would create five to seven short pieces on a topic using various genres of their own choosing. Cyrene and Lisa started by immersing students in various genres they might use for their finished projects—memoir, poetry, and op-ed.

For a long time Ryan had been interested in Riceville, Maine, a small abandoned village. He was delighted when he learned that he could use Riceville as the topic of his multigenre project. As Ryan researched the town of Riceville he dug up many primary sources: old photographs, maps, newspaper articles, even original deeds for properties there. I asked him how he was able to locate these artifacts (see an example in Figure 10.1).

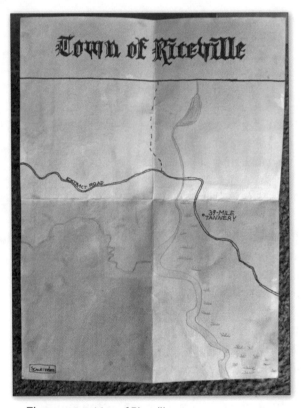

Figure 10.1 Map of Riceville

"At first I used search engines such as Google to track down information I otherwise wouldn't have known where to find," Ryan says. "Over time I stumbled on alternate sources: the registry of deeds, map archives, public libraries in other parts of the state, the Maine State Archives, and so on. So I learned where to locate specific types of resources. I also use Google Books and the Hathi Trust for accessing print information that has fallen into public domain due to age."

The material Ryan found really got him jazzed.

"It definitely helped motivate me to look for more. It's exciting to be able to assemble multiple sources into something of a big puzzle."

Historians call the kind of artifacts Ryan dug up *primary sources.* This term, as defined by Wikipedia, is used to describe "original materials that have not been altered or distorted in any way . . . In the study of history as an academic discipline, a primary source (also called *original source* or *evidence*) is an artifact, a document, a recording, or other source of information that was created at the time under study. It serves as an original source of information about the topic" (https://en.wikipedia.org/wiki/Primary_source).

When a researcher uncovers a relevant primary source it feels like striking a vein of gold. Author Russell Freedman described his feeling of profound awe when he got to hold a letter penned by Abraham Lincoln, written on translucent parchment paper.

"I truly felt like I was touching history," Freedman recalls.

Larry Dane Brimner, the author of many nonfiction books for young readers, talks about the importance of primary sources in bringing alive a historical time or place for his readers.

"Instead of creating a world for the fictional characters to live in, the nonfiction author is given that world, a cast of characters (real people)," Brimner tells me. "But the dialogue, thoughts, and emotions of those characters must be factual and sourced. To collect this information, the nonfiction author must turn to primary sources—newspapers, diaries, letters, autobiographies, etc." (See Figure 10.2.)

Figure 10.2 Classroom Connection
Introducing Primary Sources

Try introducing the idea of primary sources by having your students do a Mind Walk. Have them record everything they do during a twenty-four-hour period. Then have them respond to the following questions:

1. Which of your activities were most likely to leave behind trace evidence? (*Trace evidence* is something physical that a future researcher might find.)
2. What, if any, evidence might be preserved for the future? Why?
3. What might be left out of a historical record of your activities? Why?
4. What would a future historian be able to tell about your life and your society based on the trace evidence of your activities?
5. What are the benefits/advantages of primary sources? What are their limitations?

Note: This idea was suggested by Larry Dane Brimner, author of *Birmingham Sunday* (2010) and *Black & White: The Confrontation Between Reverend Fred L. Shuttlesworth and Eugene "Bull" Connor* (2011).

Atasi Das, who teaches fifth grade in Westminster, Vermont, has found primary sources to be invaluable in her classroom.

"I use primary sources to encourage inquiry and questioning," Atasi says. "Often I provide primary sources in the form of photographs. We use visual thinking strategies to ask, What do you notice? What do you think about this? What more could we find?"

A primary source requires the viewer to engage his or her powers of observation and interpretation. Using them encourages students to take a more active stance.

"At times we use videos, songs, and poetry to get a notion of a time, place, and/or struggle," Atasi says. "I've shown students parts of documentary movies that show human conditions and ways people work to change their lives from places like Chiapas (from *A Place Called Chiapas*) and Black Mesa on the Navajo reservation (from *Broken Rainbow*). I've also used historical census records and the official documents of immigrant ships from Europe to look at which colonies different groups of people settled and why. In all these cases, students ask questions to dig deeper into one aspect of the topic.

"This picture of the Ishango bone (Figure 10.3) is from what is known today as the Democratic Republic of Congo," Atasi says. "There is evidence that the concept of prime numbers or the use of it was recorded on this bone. Some researchers say that it might have been a woman recording her cycle. We used this at the beginning of the year in math as a way to connect how people have used various tools to make sense of the world and to reinforce the idea that we are all mathematicians."

Figure 10.3 Ishango bone artifact

An interaction with a primary source is visceral, sensory, and raw. Usually there's no filter between the individual and the artifact, no dispassionate narrator to interpret this raw data. Some teachers have found it useful to show students primary sources from two different perspectives. This can stimulate lively discussion, but it can also create disorientation in the young learner. Some researchers have found that students show discomfort with controversy when faced with more than one source showing multiple perspectives (Cohen 2009): Source A directly contradicts Source B. Which one should I believe?

After his success in digging up articles while researching the town of Riceville, Ryan had to decide how to present his material. It's not surprising that for his multigenre project Ryan decided to present a series of artifacts: a map, letters, newspaper reports, and old photographs (Figure 10.4).

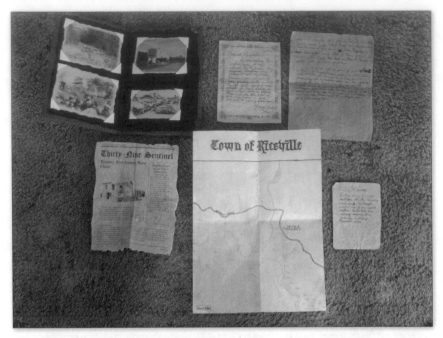

Figure 10.4 Ryan's Riceville artifacts

"The photos are forged," he told me. "They were created from elements of existing photos and other pictures that I found on the Internet. There are two photos I did not modify (only color changes): the photo of the road with ruts (I took that in April 2012 at the site of the road to Riceville), and the picture of the men sitting on the hides (a picture I found from some old Western tannery town). The other two were heavily Photoshopped."

Soon after Ryan completed this project he created an impressive website, the Abandonment of Maine (http://www.abandonmentofmaine. com), dedicated to "exploring the wilderness and forgotten places of Maine." The site includes a series of narrated videos, guidelines for explorations, and photographs. You can even buy Abandonment of Maine T-shirts. Ryan credits the multigenre research project he did in eighth grade with inspiring him to create his website.

Chapter 11

CASE HISTORY NO. 1: THE ABC'S OF BUBBLE GUM

hat does exemplary nonfiction writing look like in the classroom? What structures, routines, and conditions foster strong writing in this genre? Let's start by looking at "A Little More Than the ABC's of Bubble Gum" (Figure 11.1). The author is Caroline Andros, a fourth-grade student at the Lovett School in Atlanta, Georgia.

This piece strikes me as a great example of what student nonfiction should look and feel like. Caroline takes a mundane topic—something we take for granted—and makes it interesting, a hallmark of a skilled writer. It's studded with interesting facts, but the writing never gets bogged down. It's lively, chatty, and full of voice. Caroline is comfortable enough to include humor and wordplay. The piece is well organized and has a pleasing visual format. The photographs and drawings enhance the experience of reading it.

But when I read Caroline's piece I realized that what I held in my hands was the end of the story. I needed to rewind the video, to deconstruct the process in order to better grasp a context for how this piece got written. To do so I interviewed both Caroline and her fourth-grade teacher, Mary Lou Williams.

Ralph to Mary Lou: What's your philosophy about choice? Do you encourage students to choose their own topics?

Mary Lou: For informational writing I think writers should choose their own topic. It's really important for writers to be passionate, or at least excited about, the writing possibilities

A Little More Than The ABC's of Bubble Gum

What is bubble gum?

Bubble gum is something that everyone can use. Some people say that it helps them concentrate. Bubble gum is a small bite sized item. Bubble gum is related to chewing gum, but of course, like in the name, you can blow bubbles with it.

Some people agree and some people disagree on how bubble gum should be used. There are many different brands competing to get customers. They compete with different flavors, colors, and just how big of a bubble you can blow with it. Like the picture seen above, bubble gum comes in all different colors and flavors.

The history of bubble gum is very interesting. Many people chew bubble gum. As you can see in the POP FACT, the US certainly chews a lot of bubble gum!

Don't think that bubble gum is just some big "WOW" factor that someone just invented; it has been changed over and over again, just like technology changes. If you are a kid or when you were a kid, did you ever hear you parents say, "Don't chew that gum, it could get stuck in your hair!" or "That could get stuck on the furniture!" Well, that's all true; it will stick on most anything it touches! I still totally recommend chewing gum. You will find out that it can actually be quite good for you!

POP FACTS

In the USA alone, stores have sold 3.5 million miles of bubble gum sticks. That would be enough gum to go to the moon and back seven times!

Figure 11.1 Caroline's nonfiction writing piece

surrounding their subject. It's got to be their vision. The writer must be motivated or he or she won't really take ownership of the writing process and experience gratification once the piece is published. That's a must for building inspiration for the next piece.

Ralph to Caroline: Do you prefer to choose your own topic to write about, or do you like it when your teacher assigns you to write about a particular topic?

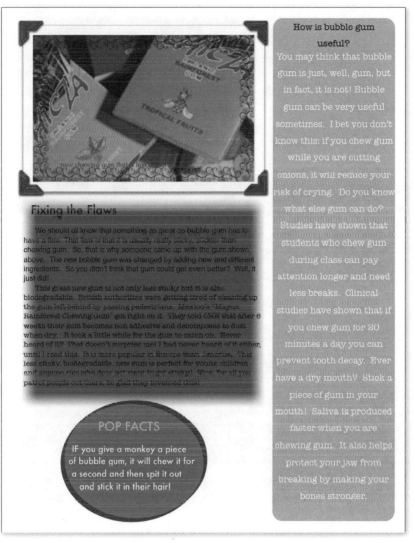

Figure 11.1 Caroline's nonfiction writing piece (continued)

Caroline: Choosing my own topic. When I get to choose my own topic, I can write about something that I am really passionate about and that I enjoy researching.

Ralph to Caroline: How did you pick this topic? What drew you to the idea of writing about bubble gum in the first place?

Caroline: Candy and gum are two things that I love! I wanted to write about something creative and fun. I really enjoy things

Bubble gum is sticky business!

WHY THIS?

Have you ever wondered why bubble gum is pink? Or why it is called "bubble gum" and why they made it so you can blow bubbles with it? Well, the reason it was pink was because it was the only color left in the factory! I guess it just stuck (get it?)! Why are Hubba Bubba and Double Bubble so successful and why do they taste soooo good? It's simple; they learned from other companies' mistakes like "Blibber Blubber." Blibber Blubber was too sticky and too tasteless for the customers. Did you know that the authorities said that it was too sticky to sell? Not only did the people dislike it, but the company was not even allowed to sell it! I hope you've enjoyed learning these crazy and zany things about bubble gum!

History THAT WILL STICK

Before the tasty bubble gum you know today, bubble gum was much different. The Ancient Greeks chewed gum from the resin in mastic trees. They called it Mastiche. Another thing they chewed was chicle, which is sap from a Sapodillia tree. People had trouble finding the prefect tasty bubble gum recipe for years and years. Finally, someone came up with the first gum in a long time, in 1848. His name was John B. Curtis. He sold "spruce" gum named State of Main Pure Spruce Gum. Two years later, Curtis discovered that flavored paraffin sold better than spruce gums.

paraffin |ˈparəfin|

noun (also **paraffin wax**) a flammable, whitish, translucent, waxy solid consisting of a mixture of saturated hydrocarbons, obtained by distillation from petroleum or shale and used in candles, cosmetics, polishes, and sealing and waterproofing compounds.

(From the New Oxford Dictionary)

He also discovered that the flavored gum tasted better (Obviously!). Curtis did not start a full "blown" company though, the first one to do that was William Finley Simple. The company was formed on December 28, 1869.

Figure 11.1 Caroline's nonfiction writing piece (continued)

that pop, and stand out. I had heard that there was an interesting story about how bubble gum was created. I wanted to learn more about the process and the history.

Ralph to Mary Lou: Do you spend time immersing students in models of strong nonfiction writing before they try writing their own?

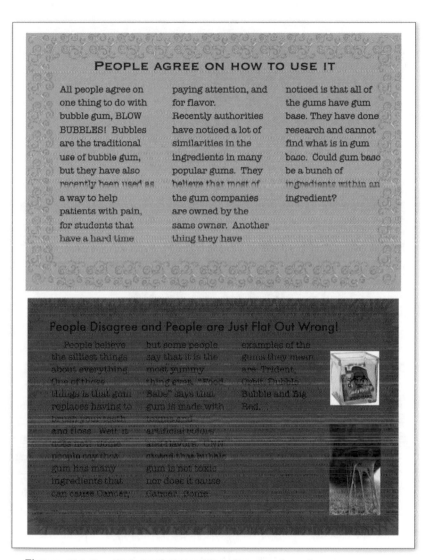

PEOPLE AGREE ON HOW TO USE IT

All people agree on one thing to do with bubble gum, BLOW BUBBLES! Bubbles are the traditional use of bubble gum, but they have also recently been used as a way to help patients with pain, for students that have a hard time paying attention, and for flavor. Recently authorities have noticed a lot of similarities in the ingredients in many popular gums. They believe that most of the gum companies are owned by the same owner. Another thing they have noticed is that all of the gums have gum base. They have done research and cannot find what is in gum base. Could gum base be a bunch of ingredients within an ingredient?

People Disagree and People are Just Flat Out Wrong!

People believe the silliest things about everything. One of these things is that gum replaces having to brush your teeth and floss. Well it does not. Some people say that gum has many ingredients that can cause Cancer. but some people say that it is the most yummy thing ever. "Food Babe" says that gum is made with toxins and artificial colors. CNN stated that bubble gum is not toxic nor does it cause Cancer. Some examples of the gums they mean are Trident, Orbit, Dubble Bubble and Big Red.

Figure 11.1 Caroline's nonfiction writing piece (continued)

Mary Lou: Oh, yes. To kick off our nonfiction study we literally wallow in mentor texts! I start out the lesson with the students sitting around me, and we discuss how nonfiction differs from other genres. I prepare five stacks of nonfiction mentor texts in advance. These stacks mostly consist of periodicals and high-interest books. It is important for the mentor texts to be very kid-friendly: *Boys' Life, American Girl, Storyworks, TIME for Kids,*

Figure 11.1 Caroline's nonfiction writing piece (continued)

and *National Geographic for Kids* are my mainstays. I also throw in high-interest books and guides such as *That's Gross, 100 Most Awesome Things on the Planet, Mysteries and Marvels of Science,* Animal Planet's *River Monsters, Body Baddies,* Eyewitness Books— *Mythology, Exploding Ants,* and more. I use a lot of gross, weird, and unusual topics. That's how I reel in the boys!

One other thing: I believe that it's important to have lots of nonfiction sources like these around the room for casual reading throughout the year. Then, armed with chart paper and enthusiasm, I model how the students can filter through a stack of mentor texts looking for two things:

1. What form (containers) does nonfiction take?

2. Did my grazing lead to a topic or idea for a topic?

As I'm chatting about my noticings and inspirations from those nonfiction texts I make two separate lists: Containers and Topics. Then I turn my writers loose. Each group wades through their stack, recording possible containers and nonfiction topics in their writer's notebooks. The area quickly gets messy, and there is a lot of sharing and conversation. I actually challenge them to see which group can record the most containers.

Later, we regroup and I make a list of nonfictional formats based on my writers' findings: feature article (the most popular), now/then, biography, newsletter/newspaper, compare/contrast, question/answer, profile, help/advice column, fact/fable, etc.

Ralph to Mary Lou: So you push them to see how many different kinds of nonfiction forms/formats they can find?

Mary Lou: Yes. Young writers need to see/experience all the different ways that nonfiction exists. I try to present this mini-lesson like a treasure hunt. I even have them take it home and look for more examples with their families. Kids have brought in Bible passages, recipes, and instructional manuals . . . I hope that some students are more excited about embracing a new container than a topic. Their next step is to figure out a topic that fits this container or how they want their writing to look.

Ralph to Caroline: Mrs. Williams mentioned that you guys read lots of mentor texts to help you write nonfiction and give you an idea what good nonfiction looks and feels and sounds like. Do you find this kind of reading to be helpful?

Caroline: Yes, I do find mentor texts helpful in many ways. Mentor texts can give you a good idea for formatting and for the way the text is written. It's helpful to know how long each thought should be and how much you should put into each section. Mrs. Williams gives us a good foundation with lots of examples and then she encourages us to use our own ideas.

Ralph to Caroline: Was there any book or article that you found particularly helpful in writing this piece? I don't just mean your research . . . I mean a nonfiction book you read where you said to yourself, "Wow, I want to do that in my writing."

Caroline: I definitely liked the *TIME for Kids* the best of the books we used to help get writing ideas. I think all of the kids enjoyed it the most and found it most helpful. It was helpful during formatting and writing text. I liked how the formatting really popped out at you.

Ralph to Mary Lou: Can you talk about focus? Do you feel the need to help your students focus what they're writing about?

Mary Lou: Yes, I help my students to narrow down their topics. One way I do that is by encouraging them to run their ideas by their parents.

Ralph to Mary Lou: Why?

Mary Lou: I think it's important for young writers to unpack their ideas and/or writing possibilities *out loud.* I also encourage my students to share/generate or rehearse their ideas with each other. This is important work that must come before research- ing and writing. (Oftentimes students who don't give their topic enough thought have to start over.) Some potentially great ideas may not be so great when they start to really think about how this topic will play out. Is it too broad? Was it chosen for effect, not substance? Is there enough information that I can under- stand out there? Maybe a writer has several terrific ideas. Trying them out on their families helps them narrow down to that one topic that resonates the most.

   Sharing writing ideas out loud reinforces the thoughts behind choosing the topic, the vocabulary, the sense of direction, and gives rise to uncovering more ways to approach and/or write about the topic. I want my students to try out their writing on their families. Yes, the families may add to their bank of ideas—well, okay. It is still the student's job to do the writing. Sometimes this instills more confidence. This translates into taking more owner- ship. Writers need to learn the thinking process that comes before and/or with the prewriting phase. They've got to be good envision- ers too. (By the way, once my writers say, "I'm finished with my piece," I have them read the piece out loud several more times. They always find errors, and actually get excited about that!)

Ralph to Mary Lou: While students are starting to research, collecting their material, and writing, do you do mini-lessons about craft elements for nonfiction?

Mary Lou: Yes. The students are always excited about getting the piece started, so I don't want to hold them back. I turn them loose and then sprinkle in lessons as they're working.

Ralph to Mary Lou: What kind of lessons do you do?

Mary Lou: The hook is so important, so I make a really big deal out of them. We hunt for great hooks in the stacks, and I have them try out several different ways.

I do lessons that review comma work: compound sentences, introductory phrases, listing commas, quotation marks, and appositive phrases. I make sure to do a lesson on transition words. I show my students how to use a thesaurus to pump up their word choice. I remind my writers about vague use of pronouns. This is big!

I like to use their draft work for lessons. They love this, and it makes these lessons more meaningful. As a class, we may look for places where transition words would be helpful, or show how whatever is the focus can be reworked in the piece to make it more effective. I also use polished pieces from previous years to make a point. And we talk about the importance of layouts and how digital tools can support the text in meaningful ways.

Ralph: I noticed that your students write with voice. They sound like kids. That's unusual—often student nonfiction sounds limp and voiceless, just a list of facts. How do you encourage students to write nonfiction with voice?

Mary Lou: I tell them, "Take it seriously but be yourself. Pack a punch! Make sure your audience knows that you are informed and what you are sharing is important." I keep reiterating that you've got to make your audience understand that there is power in writing and you are the force behind that power. Impress me!

Ralph: I believe that students can write nonfiction with fluency and confidence when they have depth of knowledge about their topics. How do you help your students build that depth of knowledge?

Mary Lou: First of all, my students must feel strongly about the topic AND want to learn more. This may mean acknowledging that their initial topic wasn't so good after all, and starting over again.

Researching is still very much a developing skill for kids this age, so I need to model it. I choose a topic and walk them through how I would research, save, and chunk out that information prior to the drafting. The prewriting is a must. No one starts typing until the prewriting is complete and approved. That doesn't mean it's necessarily good, but it is a plan that covers the hook/intro, body, and conclusion. The writing grows from there.

Ralph to Caroline: I wanted to ask you about organization. I notice that you use subheadings in your writing. How did you decide to do that? Did you set up that organization early in the research process . . . or later when you started to write?

Caroline: Before I started writing, I made a list of the way that I wanted the order of the text to go. Then, I took what I put for the headings in my list and I put them on top of my text and wrote about that topic as I went. I like subheadings because they give the reader an idea of what they are going to read about before they start that section.

Ralph to Caroline: Where did you get the idea for Pop Facts?

Caroline: When I was doing my research I found some really interesting facts that wouldn't go in any of my subheadings. So, I decided to make a "Fun Facts" section. I decided to call it "Pop Facts" because I thought that went along with my topic more and made it more interesting.

Ralph to Mary Lou: How does audience fit into nonfiction writing?

Mary Lou: Students at this age tend to put themselves first. What do I like? What do I want? How do I feel? So . . . how does your writing work with your audience? This is an important question that students need to consider, but they have to understand what it means first. They need to understand that a good writer can hook and capture his audience regardless of the topic. I want my writers to always be thinking about that. What can I do to move, excite, and/or challenge my audience?

Ralph to Mary Lou: How do your students share/publish their nonfiction pieces?

Mary Lou: They may share their favorite parts or what they learned through research with the class. The polished pieces are printed in color and showcased in the hall. The students love to read (and compare) what was written on the grade level. I am currently setting up a digital portfolio on our class website. I am going to ask the students to share what inspired them to write the pieces and/or why they chose the topics. Parents will be able to comment on the work. I think that the teacher's level of enthusiasm is a key ingredient.

Ralph to Mary Lou: Can you say more about that?

Mary Lou: If the teacher isn't enthusiastic, why should the students be enthusiastic? I feel like a coach. It doesn't make any difference if we are talking about math, writing, social studies, or at recess. Students respond best to enthusiasm, confidence, and a can-do attitude. Flexibility and spontaneity are essentials. The level of motivation is determined by attitude. Not every writer is going to be a great writer—that's okay—but all writers can work toward their next level and feel good about their accomplishment. When a writer sees self-improvement, he or she is more enthusiastic and inspired to tackle that next piece.

Implications and Take-Aways

The comments and insights I received from Caroline and her teacher allowed me to peek behind the curtain and better understand how Caroline was able to create such a wonderful piece of nonfiction. As I reflect on the interviews, I can see several important principles that are worth highlighting:

- **Sustained immersion in mentor texts.** Mary Lou and her students spent class time looking closely at the "what" (content) and the "how" (format) of multiple texts. This helped students build vision for nonfiction.
- **Balance of guidance and freedom.** Mary Lou wanted her students to choose their own topics and gave them a great deal of guidance along the way.
- **Time.** The whole process took three or four weeks. Mary Lou didn't rush the process—she gave her students ample time to enter into this experience.

Two small caveats: First, I'm wary of overreliance on prewriting. Formalized prewriting can feel like a straitjacket, especially to boys, who may want more freedom to create their own formats in an invent-as-you-go manner. Still, Mary Lou swears by it, and Caroline indicated to me that she found it helpful to plan out her piece ahead of time.

I'm ambivalent about the idea of directing kids to share their ideas with their parents. Mary Lou gives several compelling reasons for doing so, though I do wonder if overzealous parents might be tempted to co-create the piece of nonfiction—that is, write it for the student.

But these quibbles are minor. Mary Lou Williams has a depth of knowledge about nonfiction, and knows how to structure her class so her students can profit from it. She gives her students a balance of guidance and freedom, and they flourish in that environment. Caroline's bubble gum piece provides convincing evidence of that fact.

Chapter 12

CASE HISTORY NO. 2: KINDERGARTEN ETHNOGRAPHIES

Bob Crongeyer teaches at Taylor Street School in Sacramento, California. Recently he led his fifth- and sixth-grade students through a class nonfiction project in which they studied kindergarten children and wrote ethnographies about them. He kicked off the project by reading aloud Madeleine L'Engle's *A Wrinkle in Time*. This sparked a class discussion and led to the question "Is Charles Wallace a typical five-year-old child?" After some basic research, the class decided that the field of anthropology would offer the best way to answer this question.

Educator Sandra Kaplan has influenced Bob's thinking as a teacher. One of the basic premises of Kaplan's work is that if we want students to learn about geology they need to think like geologists. Study the weather? Have them think like meteorologists, and so on.

"Dr. Sandra Kaplan suggests that students are used to 'thinking like disciplinarians,'" Bob told me. "So it wasn't a stretch to have them find out what being an anthropologist entailed."

To introduce students to ethnographic writing, Bob drew on a variety of mentor texts, including several YouTube videos. One was a *60 Minutes* segment about Jane Goodall; another was an introduction to anthropology. Bob showed these videos in class, and his students took notes. From those resources, they began to get a feel for the processes and tools an anthropologist might use.

These videos also spurred a debate about an ethics question: Should an anthropologist interact with his or her subjects? Bob asked his students to write their preliminary thoughts in their journals ahead of time. Then they had a class discussion, which clarified their thinking. In the end they decided that, yes, they could interact with their subjects, but only after they had observed once or twice before. I asked Bob if he talked to his students about ethnographic research, or structured it in any way.

"Before our first visit to the kindergarten class we discussed and practiced how to take notes without bias," Bob said. "For instance, I explained that they shouldn't write 'Two friends were playing with each other,' but rather 'Two males were chasing each other near the play structure.' They learned to write what they observed, not what they expected to observe." (That's helpful advice for any nonfiction writer.)

Bob's students visited the kindergarten class on three separate occasions. Some of his students brought binoculars as well as their journals; some took some video footage. After each session they reflected on their experiences by writing in their journals. This was the one time they could include as much personal opinion as they wanted.

At this point Bob introduced the word *ethnography* to the class. He explained that ethnography is one way anthropologists can report what they've discovered. Bob knew it would be important for his students to have an image for what ethnography looks and sounds like. He learned that Randy Hodson, a sociology professor at Ohio State, had posted some ethnography papers by his students online. Bob had read them and thought they offered good examples of strong ethnographic writing, so he decided to print them out and use them with his students as mentor texts. Here's a link:

http://www.thesummitprep.org/pmisterovich/files/2011/11/Soc-101-Ethnographic-Study-Examples-2011.pdf. (Note: Bob did not use the paper on subcultures with his students.)

"I did have to censor some of the more colorful language (in the papers written by the college students)," Bob says, "but most of them were perfectly appropriate. They showed my students a variety of structures and writing styles that accomplished the writers' goals of reporting their findings. And my students definitely thought it was cool to be reading college papers!"

The students worked in groups to analyze the beginnings of the papers (see Figures 12.1–12.4). Then they wrote beginnings to their own ethnographies (see excerpt in Figure 12.5). Some focused on the setting, their observations, their preconceived notions, or their feelings about the project.

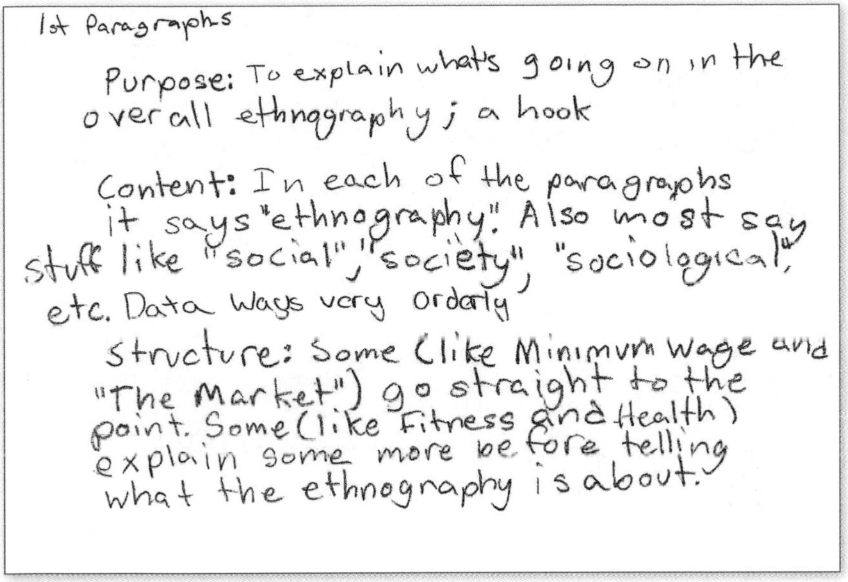

1st Paragraphs

Purpose: To explain what's going on in the overall ethnography; a hook

Content: In each of the paragraphs it says "ethnography". Also most say stuff like "social", "society", "sociological", etc. Data was very orderly

Structure: Some (like Minimum Wage and "The Market") go straight to the point. Some (like Fitness and Health) explain some more before telling what the ethnography is about.

Figure 12.1 Student analysis of mentor texts

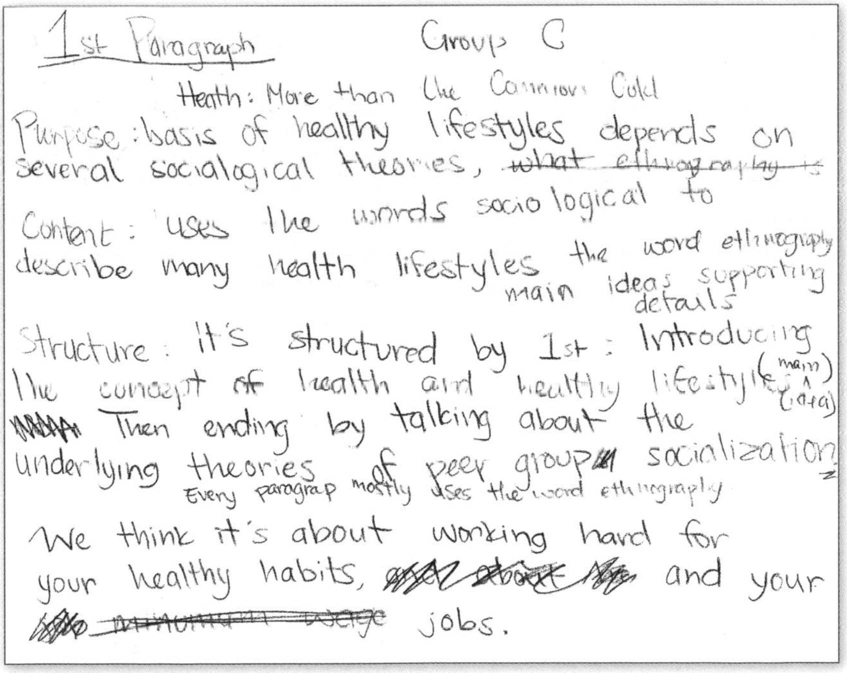

1st Paragraph   Group C

Health: More than the Common Cold

Purpose: basis of healthy lifestyles depends on several sociological theories, ~~what ethnography is~~

Content: uses the words socio logical to describe many health lifestyles   the word ethnography
                                                        main   ideas supporting
                                                                    details

Structure: It's structured by 1st: Introducing
the concept of health and healthy lifestyle (main)
~~xxxx~~ Then ending by talking about the   (data)
underlying theories of peer group socialization
        Every paragraph mostly uses the word ethnography

We think it's about working hard for
your healthy habits, ~~xxxx xxxx xxxx~~ and your
~~xxxx xxxx xxxx~~ jobs.

Figure 12.2 Student analysis of mentor texts

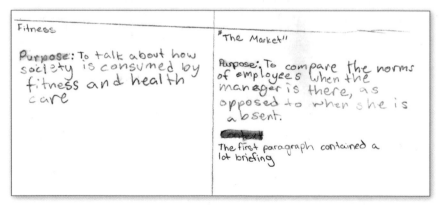

1st PARAGRAPHS

Structure
- Most ovi them has titles
- Most topic sentences are the first sentence, and one is the third sentence

Content
- all have to do with society
- every paper has the word ethnography

Purpose
- the purpose is to introduce the main idea

Fitness

Purpose: To talk about how society is consumed by fitness and health care

"The Market"

Purpose: To compare the norms of employees when the manager is there, as opposed to when she is absent.

Context
The first paragraph contained a lot briefing

Figures 12.3 (above) and 12.4 (below) Student analyses of mentor texts

The whole process for these ethnographies—including mini-lessons, research, and writing time—took about a month. I asked Bob if he talked to his students about audience. Did they have a sense of whom they were writing for?

"Yes, after our third session I asked them what we should do with our data," Bob explained. "Most of them felt that they had more than enough information to answer our initial question. They realized that their observational data would be interesting and maybe even useful to the kindergarten teachers. Because they had different perspectives, they also wanted to share their findings with each other. So there were at least two audiences they were writing for."

Implications and Take-Aways

Bob's students underwent a rich experience in writing their kindergarten ethnographies. This nonfiction project may sound a bit exotic, but it does reveal some important characteristics of strong nonfiction learning.

- **Scope.** The students in Bob's class knew that they weren't doing itty-bitty reports or stale schoolwork. The ethnography project was big, serious, and ambitious. These students were trying to follow in the legendary footsteps of Jane Goodall. This is a fine example of project learning. The writing does not generate the energy; rather, the wider project, with all its associated activities, gets kids excited, which, in turn, leads to strong writing.
- **Choice?** In Bob's class project the topic was predetermined. He had a clear goal—he wanted to challenge his students to write their own ethnographies of kindergarten students. Student choice played out within the parameters of the project. Could there have been more choice? I wonder what would have happened if students had been given more leeway, perhaps being allowed to choose their own subjects for their ethnographies?
- **Social, not solitary.** "This project had a lot to do with socializing," says Hannah, a student in Bob's class. "Other projects I've done had more to do with concentrating and desk work, which was a lot less social."

    Too often nonfiction writing is a solitary endeavor. In Bob's class much of the work was interpersonal and collaborative. As his kids read the college ethnographies they put their heads together and talked about what those students tried to do. They interviewed the kindergarten students. I made this point earlier but it's worth repeating: not all students will enter the world of

A Wrinkle in Norms

Ethnographic Studies Reveal Typical Behavior
of Kindergarten Students

Compiled by Taylor Street School's
GATE Scholars
2013

Figure 12.5 (above and opposite) An excerpt from the class's completed ethnographies

Kindergartners

For my ethnography project I decided to go see kindergartners in their natural habitat. I'll include an interview with one of the kindergartners. The main focus about this ethnography is how the kindergartners act when their inside class and outside at recess.

In their class they color, draw, and learn interesting things. One game they play is called rhyming. There would be cards on the floor and the kindergartners would try to find rhymes like cat, hat and mouse, house.

What really surprised me is that the kindergartners pay attention to the teacher. I thought that they would be naughty, not paying attention,and playing around.

At recess I saw two kids parallel playing. Parallel playing is when kids are next to another but not interacting with each other.

The kindergartner I interviewed is Kaelan. She is five years old, likes the color pink, loves to watch Dora, and likes to sing the alphabet.

Throughout this study I think that the kindergartners good inside class and outside at recess. Even though their small they all have big personalities.

business, but the ones who do will likely be required to work—think, synthesize, write—in a team setting. Collaborative writing skills are increasingly valuable in the workplace.

- **Crucial role of mentor texts.** Bob had to familiarize his students with a new and somewhat difficult genre, but he didn't rely on premade rubrics or anchor texts. Rather, he asked his students to study authentic pieces that exist in the world beyond the walls of a school building. In other words, the students were doing life work, not just schoolwork.

    I wanted Bob's students to reflect on the process of writing their ethnographies, so we asked them the question "How did your reading and viewing (*A Wrinkle in Time*, the college papers, and the Jane Goodall video) make it easier for you to write about the kindergarten kids?" Here are some of their responses:

    o "Seeing the structure of another paper written out, and working with another text, helped me because I am dyslexic and oftentimes I need to see things written out or do them for myself."

    o "Those books and film and stuff helped us learn more vocabulary that scientists use when they study things."

    o "They helped me to write more sophisticated. And they helped us get the main idea of how our ethnographies should flow."

    o "They made the process easier because those resources displayed examples that we could gain knowledge from. *They helped our brains ease into ethnographies: their structures, purpose, contexts, etc.*" (italics mine)

- **Use of fiction.** Like Penny Kittle (see Chapter 8), Bob believed it would be important for his students to read both nonfiction and fiction texts. Reading fiction requires a leap of the imagination, which is necessary for all kinds of writing—including nonfiction.
- **Humor and voice.** While the students were faithful to the form, they also felt comfortable enough to incorporate sly humor into their pieces. I take humor to be one of the most reliable indicators that a student is comfortable, confident, and knows her material through and through.

- **Incorporation of narrative elements.** The best ethnographies in Bob's class had all the elements of compelling stories, complete with finely observed character, plot, setting, and conflict—and quirky detail.

- **Multiple formats.** It's true that the student papers emulated ethnographic writing, but students also incorporated other formats: interviews, lists, artifacts (autographs written by the kindergarten students), and anecdotes.

- **Presence of a highly skilled teacher.** The students did the actual research and writing, of course, but Bob structured this project in such a way that ensured they would have success. He provided the right balance of class study and independent work. He didn't expect or want formulaic writing; rather, he made space for his students to put the stamp of their personalities on their finished product. He didn't rush them through this unit. Rather, he understood that his students would need sustained time to become comfortable with a new genre and succeed in it. He established a sense of seriousness in that classroom and set high standards. That's what first-class teaching looks like.

Chapter 13

DEGLAZING THE PAN: DOS, DON'TS, AND PRACTICAL TIPS FOR TEACHING NONFICTION

Nonfiction is a broad genre that encompasses expository writing, academic writing, and writing across the curriculum, just to name a few. Those areas, while important, lie outside the scope of this book. In this book I'm focusing on nonfiction as information writing. I hope to use this final chapter as a kind of reduction sauce that concentrates on the issues I consider most important for teaching nonfiction.

Use the Writing Workshop Structure for Nonfiction Writing

There's no need to reinvent the wheel and force kids to relearn a whole new structure when they delve into this genre. Build on familiarity. You'll find the writing workshop structure to be more than adequate:

Mini-lesson—Devote this time to sharing mentor texts and craft elements for nonfiction.

Writing time—Kids will be researching, gathering, drafting. You'll move around the class conferring with individual students, wherever they are in their process.

Share—Your students may not be ready to share finished pieces, at least at first, but they can share their process—what they are learning, surprises, what problems they are running into, etc.

Choice Leads to Voice in Writing

We all know what can happen when a student finds a "just-right" book. But a similar magic occurs when a student can choose a *just-right topic*—that is, one they are passionate about.

Every teacher has at least one reluctant writer. How do you get that kid motivated to write? The trick is to find out what he or she is most interested in (obsessed with), and encourage the student to write about that.

Open up choice and see what happens. There's no reason why nonfiction must be confined to a unit of study. Consider having an "open unit" every so often where students get to choose both the genre (poetry, fiction, nonfiction, etc.) *and* topic (e.g., baseball, jellyfish, being one of a set of triplets). This is an important and powerful opportunity for kids to find out what it feels like to follow seed ideas from their notebooks to the most appropriate form, including nonfiction. You'll be surprised by the lively buzz in the class when this happens. And you'll notice a kind of cross-pollination where kids writing in one genre will be intrigued and inspired by those who are writing in another.

Beware of Formulaic Nonfiction

Last year a fifth-grade teacher read my book *Fig Pudding* to the class. Afterward the students wrote letters to me. After reading the third one I began to notice a suspicious similarity in each letter I read. The students would tell me what they liked in the first paragraph; in the second paragraph they shared connections to their own lives; in the third they asked me questions about the book. Lo and behold, attached to the very last letter I found a Xeroxed sheet titled *FIG PUDDING* LETTER RUBRIC. The kids were following a predetermined format. No wonder all those letters sounded the same.

When student nonfiction writing all begins to sound the same, a little bell should go off in our heads that tells us something is wrong. It's not pleasurable to read a batch of identical student writing samples. I have always loved the title of Linda Rief's book *Seeking Diversity* (1991). That's what we want—students who can express their own unique voices. I want the writing to be different and diverse.

A well-known educator, someone I highly respect, disagrees with me on this point and told me, "In fact, I think you lead with structure when you teach nonfiction."

To this I replied, "Well, you could lead with structure, but couldn't you also lead with voice? Or anger? Or story?" And even if I concede the point that we should lead with structure (which I don't), why must we always lead with the same structure that every student must follow? Why not allow students to experiment with various structures and let them find the one that best fits what they're writing about (as I did when I decided to use a parable in Chapter 1 to get my point across)?

I believe we need to rethink form when our students write nonfiction. If we do, we'll be embracing the changes in evolving and creative nonfiction we increasingly find in the world at large.

Don't Skimp on Mentor Texts

In the previous chapter we met Bob Crongeyer and his sixth-grade students who wrote kindergarten ethnographies last year. Bob looped with his students, so he has the same kids in seventh grade. This year he wanted them to do something different.

"I had just finished a series of mini-lessons on argumentative writing that led to some interesting discoveries," Bob told me. "I followed lessons from a National Writing Project, but soon realized we hadn't looked at any mentor texts, which I usually do when getting my kids to write in a certain genre. The writing they produced sounded clunky. Their papers didn't flow. So we went back and did a genre study for writing an argument."

Writing can only be as good as the literature that supports, surrounds, and buoys it up. Finding strong mentor texts is a task that doesn't have to fall solely on the teacher—have kids look for great nonfiction, too.

Don't Overdo Prewriting

I think those educators who lean heavily on prewriting view writers as people with a singular approach. First they plan it out. After that, they execute the plan. But what about those writers who invent as they go, who figure it out along the way?

At the beginning of this book I stated that nonfiction is the genre most typically "done to" students. Often we give them elaborate outlines and direct them to follow the outline. Such outlines often lead to formulaic, paint-by-number writing. Kids never really get their stride and rhythm to write about their topics. But there's another problem with outlines—they make students dependent on us. The next time they attempt to write nonfiction they'll need us to first hand them another detailed outline.

Whatever prewriting students do should move them toward independence. Lucy Calkins has talked about having kids make a map rather than an outline: "A map should be good enough to work from but cheap enough to throw away." This makes sense. Students have only a finite amount of energy or "juice" for a piece of writing. I'd like to see them invest that energy in the writing itself rather than the prewrite.

Value Passion, Originality, and Voice

Strong nonfiction writing is fresh and bold, and contains an element of surprise that makes you sit up and say, hey! Consider this piece of writing about the NBA, written by Alvin, a fifth grader from Washington State.

My Basketball Opinions

The Lakers win, the Cavs always lose,
Every game the Bobcats take a snooze,
The Spurs are strong, the Celtics are tall,
Lebron James always hogs the ball.

Kevin Garnett's tough, Dwayne Wade is sly,
You can't dunk on Dwight Howard, he'll deny,
Kobe Bryant's smooth, Shaquille O'Neal's chunky,
Whenever Shannon Brown goes for a dunk
It's always funky.

Memphis sparkles with loneliness,
Boston lingers with fame,
The Nuggets and the Pistons,
No two teams are the same.

I enjoyed the rhythmic quality to the first part of Alvin's piece, but in the last stanza the first two stunning verbs bowled me over. Memphis *sparkles* with loneliness (I believe he means that the Memphis Grizzlies rarely even make the playoffs); Boston *lingers* with fame. Certainly it's playful, out-of-the-box nonfiction, but it's undeniably effective. And those two lines make this piece unforgettable.

Celebrate Edgy Writing That Makes You Sit Up and Take Notice

There's a certain kind of nonfiction that's meant to be a wake-up call, a call to action. The following piece about high-stakes testing was written by Billie L., an eighth grader. Billie has learned the power of language, how you can write one thing but mean the opposite. Her piece combines nonfiction, satire, how-to, and far-flung fantasy to create a devastating political commentary.

Severe Weather Testing Protocols

1. Should a severe weather situation occur during testing, please remain calm. To display any kind of anxiety would be a testing irregularity and must be reported.

2. Please do not look out the window to watch for approaching tornadoes. You must monitor the students at all times. To do otherwise, would be a testing irregularity and must be reported.

3. Should students notice an approaching tornado and begin to cry, please make every effort to protect their testing materials from the flow of tears and sinus drainage.

4. Should a flying object come through your window during testing, please make every effort to ensure that it does not land on a testing booklet or an answer sheet. Please make sure to soften the landing of the flying object so that it will not disturb the students while testing.

5. Should shards of glass from a broken window come flying into the room, have the students use their bodies to shield their testing materials so that they will not be damaged. Have plenty of gauze on hand to ensure that no one accidentally bleeds on the answer documents. Damaged answer sheets will not scan properly.

6. Should gale force winds ensue, please have everyone stuff their test booklets and answer sheets into their shirts . . . being very careful not to bend them because bent answer documents will not scan properly.

7. If any student gets sucked into the vortex of the funnel cloud, please make sure they mark at least one answer before departing . . . and of course make sure they leave their answer sheets and test booklets behind. You will have to account for those.

8. Should a funnel cloud pick you, the test administrator, up and take you flying over the rainbow, you will still be required to account for all of your testing materials when you land so please take extra precautions. Remember, once you have checked them out, they should never leave your hands.

9. When rescue workers arrive to dig you out of the rubble, please make sure that they do not, at any time, look at or handle the testing materials. Once you have been treated for your injuries, you will still be responsible for checking your materials back in. Search dogs will not be allowed to sift through the rubble for lost tests . . . unless of course they have been through standardized test training.

10. Please do not pray should a severe weather situation arise. Your priority is to actively monitor the test and a student might mark in the wrong section if you are praying instead of monitoring. I'm sure God will put war, world hunger, crime, and the presidential primaries on hold until testing is over. He knows how important this test is.

Years ago I saw a sculpture exhibition that featured creations constructed entirely out of car transmissions. It was titled *Art Is the Transmission of Discovery*. Clever, and a phrase that gives an apt description of nonfiction writing. First, the writer discovers the material—it must come alive in his or her imagination. Next, the writer strives to convey that sense of excitement and discovery to the reader. The best writers explain the complex world to us in a way we can understand, without dumbing it down. Equally important, they convey a sense of wonder about their subjects.

The best word to describe today's nonfiction is *dynamic*, which means "characterized by constant change, activity, or progress." We shouldn't settle for formulaic writing of any kind, particularly in a genre like nonfiction that is busy being born and reborn every day in the world at large. Let's create writing classrooms where our students can take part in the dance and embrace nonfiction in all of its rich possibilities.

References

Diane Ackerman. 1991. *A Natural History of the Senses*. New York: Knopf Doubleday.

———. 2012. *One Hundred Names for Love*. New York. W. W. Norton.

Berger, Ron. 2003 *An Ethic of Excellence: Building a Culture of Craftsmanship with Students*. Portsmouth, NH: Heinemann.

Bragg, Rick. 2002. "Olympics: Skeleton Plunges Face-First Back into the Winter Games." *New York Times*, February 17.

Cohen, Sharon. 2009. "Why Do Students Find Reading History Challenging?" *World History Connected*. http://worldhistoryconnected. press.illinois.edu/6.3/cohen.html.

Cowen, Ron. 2014. "It's Snack Time in the Cosmos." *New York Times*, February 17. http://www.nytimes.com/2014/02/18/science/its-snack-time-in-the-cosmos.html?_r=0.

Fletcher, Ralph. 2006. *Boy Writers: Reclaiming Their Voices*. Portland, ME: Stenhouse.

———. 2011. *Mentor Authors, Mentor Texts: Short Texts, Class Notes, and Practical Classroom Uses*. Portsmouth, NH: Heinemann.

Johnson, Carolyn Y. 2015. "Tiny Blackpoll Warblers Make Mind-Boggling Migration." *Boston Globe*, April 1. http://www.bostonglobe.com/metro/2015/03/31/tiny-blackpoll-warbler-makes-mind-boggling-nonstop-migration/xrfuOBZn7uo5NadrZiV1UN/story.html.

Junger, Sebastian. 2009. *The Perfect Storm: A True Story of Men Against the Sea*. New York: W. W. Norton.

Kittle, Penny. 2012. *Book Love: Developing Depth, Stamina, and Passion in Adolescent Readers*. Portsmouth, NH: Heinemann.

Laminack, Lester. 2009. *Unwrapping the Read Aloud: Making Every Read Aloud Intentional and Instructional*. New York: Scholastic.

Lane, Barry. 1992. *After "The End": Teaching and Learning Creative Revision*. Portsmouth, NH: Heinemann.

Perkins, David N. 2014. *Future Wise: Educating Our Children for a Changing World*. San Francisco: Jossey-Bass.

Pondiscio, Robert. 2012. "Worse Than Awful: An Insider's View of Educational Publishing." *The Core Knowledge Blog*. http://blog.coreknowledge.org/author/robert-pondiscio/page/6/.

Portalupi, JoAnn, and Ralph Fletcher. 2001. *Nonfiction Craft Lessons: Teaching Information Writing, K–8*. Portland, ME: Stenhouse.

Ray, Katie Wood. 2006. *Study Driven: A Framework for Planning Units of Study in the Writing Workshop*. Portsmouth, NH: Heinemann.

Rief, Linda. 1991. *Seeking Diversity*. Portsmouth, NH: Heinemann.

———. 2014. *Read Write Teach: Choice and Challenge in the Reading-Writing Workshop*. Portsmouth, NH: Heinemann.

Romano, Tom. 2000. *Blending Genre, Altering Style: Writing Multigenre Research Papers*. Portsmouth, NH: Heinemann.

———. 2013. *Fearless Writing. Multigenre to Motivate and Inspire*. Portsmouth, NH: Heinemann.

Sibberson, Franki, and Karen Szymusiak. 2003. *Still Learning to Read*. Portland, ME: Stenhouse.

Stedman, M. L. 2012. *The Light Between Oceans*. New York: Scribner.

Thomas, Evan. 2002. *Robert Kennedy: His Life*. New York: Simon and Schuster.

TIME for Kids. 1999. "A Monster Hurricane." Vol. 5, Number 3.

Weisman, Alan. 2014. "Why the Earth Is Farting." CNN News, August 12. http://www.cnn.com/2014/08/12/opinion/weisman-craters-methane/.

Zinsser, William. 1993. *Writing to Learn: How to Write and Think Clearly About Any Subject at All*. New York: HarperCollins.

Children's Books

See Chapter 6 for a list of nonfiction read-aloud suggestions.

Allen, Judy. 2004. *Are You a Bee?* Backyard Books series. New York: Kingfisher.

Borden, Louise. 1998. *Good-Bye, Charles Lindbergh: Based on a True Story*. New York: Margaret K. McElderry Books.

———. 2000. *Sleds on Boston Common: A Story from the American Revolution*. New York: Margaret K. McElderry Books.

———. 2001. *Fly High! The Story of Bessie Coleman*. New York: Margaret K. McElderry Books.

———. 2003. *The Little Ships: The Heroic Rescue at Dunkirk in World War II*. New York: Margaret K. McElderry Books.

———. 2003. *Touching the Sky: The Flying Adventures of Wilbur and Orville Wright*. New York: Margaret K. McElderry Books.

———. 2004. *The Greatest Skating Race: A World War II Story from the Netherlands*. New York: Margaret K. McElderry Books.

———. 2004. *Sea Clocks: The Story of Longitude*. New York: Margaret K. McElderry Books.

———. 2005. *The Journey That Saved Curious George: The True Wartime Escape of Margret and H. A. Rey*. Boston: HMH Books for Young Readers.

———. 2012. *His Name Was Raoul Wallenberg: Courage, Rescue, and Mystery During World War II*. Boston: HMH Books for Young Readers.

Brimner, Larry Dane. 2010. *Birmingham Sunday*. Honesdale, PA: Calkins Creek.

———. 2011. *Black & White: The Confrontation Between Reverend Fred L. Shuttlesworth and Eugene "Bull" Connor*. Honesdale, PA: Calkins Creek.

Halls, Kelly Milner. 2006. *Tales of the Cryptids: Mysterious Creatures That May or May Not Exist*. Minneapolis, MN: Darby Creek.

———. 2011. *In Search of Sasquatch.* Boston: HMH Books for Young Readers.

———. 2012. *Alien Investigation: Searching for the Truth About UFOs and Aliens.* Minneapolis, MN: Millbrook Press.

L'Engle, Madeleine. 1962. *A Wrinkle in Time.* New York: Macmillan.

Index